THE
OTHER
FACE
OF
LOVE

MIRIAM POLLARD

THE
OTHER
FACE
OF
LOVE

*Dialogues with
the Prison Experience of*

ALBERT SPEER

A Crossroad Book
The Crossroad Publishing Company
New York

Acknowledgment is gratefully extended for permission to reprint from the following:

Inside the Third Reich, by Albert Speer. Reprinted with the permission of Simon & Schuster and Weidenfeld and Nicholson, London. Translated from the German by Richard and Clara Wilson. Copyright © 1969 by Verlag Ullstein Gmbh. English translation copyright © 1970 by Macmillan Publishing Company.

Spandau: The Secret Diaries, by Albert Speer. Reprinted with the permission of Simon & Schuster. Copyright © 1975 by Verlag Ullstein Gmbh. English translation copyright © 1976 by Macmillan Publishing Company

Walter Abbott, S.J., ed., *Documents of Vatican II* (New York: America Press, 1966).

Bernard of Clairvaux, *Sermons on the Song of Songs,* vol. 3, trans. Kilian Walsh and Irene Edmonds (1979), and vol. 4, trans. Irene Edmonds (1980), published by Cistercian Publications, WMU Station, Kalamazoo, MI 49008.

Leo Tolstoy, *War and Peace* (Chicago: Encyclopaedia Britannica, Great Books ed., 1952).

New Revised Standard Version Bible, copyright 1989, Division of Christian Education of the National Council of the Churches of Christ in the United States of America.

Sculpture of Speer: Yrsa von Leistner

1996

The Crossroad Publishing Company
370 Lexington Avenue, New York, NY 10017

Copyright © 1996 by Miriam Pollard

Library of Congress Cataloging-in-Publication Data

Pollard, Miriam.
    The other face of love : dialogues with the prison experience of Albert Speer / Miriam Pollard.
      p. cm.
    ISBN 0-8245-1562-5 (hardcover)
    1. Forgiveness of sin. 2. God—Mercy. 3. Speer, Albert, 1905- — Religion. 4. Speer, Albert, 1905- Spandauer Tagebücher.
    I. Title.
    BT795.P63 1996
    234'.5–dc20   96-10685
                                                        CIP

Contents

Part III
THE TOOLS

Part IV
THE WOMEN

Part V
THE WALKER

Part VI
THE OTHERS

Part VII
THE MARBLE

Lazarus Our Friend

"Lord, if you had been here, my brother would not have died."

After a long struggle with the Lazarus story, I have come to love these lines. They are an honest way of expressing what our relationship with God is like when we feel awful, or when we stop to concentrate on even some of the least spectacular of the world's woes.

If you had been here, if you had cared, if you were any good, if you exist at all....

Faith is not a warm fire on a cold night. It's often the wind's whip and the ditch we stumbled into because the moon went out. It can be reading maps that don't go anywhere and a numbness of the brain that's trying to make sense of what refuses to make sense.

Lord, if you had been here...

It's not at all a bad prayer. It's saying to Christ that we know he's too good — or desperately hope he's too good — to want the mess we see we're stuck with.

This is a book about mercy, which is God's way of dealing with the mess we're stuck with. Mercy is what we hope is somebody else's business, a courtesy we do not want to need. But there it is. There it is at the heart of everything.

Lord, if you had been here, six million of your people would not have died under Hitler. If you had been here, five million Ukrainians would not have starved to death in Stalin's hand-made famine. Lord, remember Oscar Romero, the Disappeared, the stinking slums, the street children. Lord, if you had been here...

Are we looking for the wrong face in the crowd? Are we asking for the wrong kind of explanation? Answers can't explain. They can only answer. They lead to other questions which often intensify the darkness. "Lord, if you had been here..."

Why am I linking the misery of the world with the mercy of God? Because that's where mercy builds its house — in the barrios, in the death camps, in the moral and emotional slums of the human heart. Lord, if you had been here, my brother would not have starved, my sister would not be displayed in the shop window of a brothel in Thailand as merchandise for the tourist trade. My daughter would not be on drugs, my son would not be dying of AIDS.

The terrible way we treat one another, the monstrous roll of human history — is there anything at all that can redeem the irredeemable? Is there any way at all that we can help?

Lord, if you had been here...

The trouble is we know the answer, and our difficulty is believing what we know. We know that he was there as he is here: in the exploited, and just as surely struggling to be free in the exploiter; in the dying of the body and in the dying of the soul. We've learned that, being there, he doesn't fix things as we'd like. Mercy has its own dynamic, a dynamic operative in the humblest and most respectable of human lives, as well as in the desperate and oppressed.

The Man

And that is the why of this book. I have chosen as an archetype of mercy someone who clearly needed it, and I admire those who, having read the manuscript, say spontaneously, "That man is I." I could say the same, except I'm sure I wouldn't have done as well as he with what he had to deal with.

Albert Speer was born March 19, 1905, in Mannheim, Germany. He died of a cerebral hemorrhage September 1, 1981, in London, where he had gone to be interviewed at the request of the BBC. Of those seventy-six years, ten had been given to the service of Adolf Hitler, first as his favored architect and the designer of Nazi spectaculars, then as Minister of Armaments and War Production. The twenty years on which I largely concentrate were spent in Spandau Prison; and during the last sixteen years of his life, he shared with the world, in books and interviews, his personal experience of Nazi leadership.

He accepted responsibility for the damage Hitler's policies inflicted on the world, which means that he accepted a degree of responsibility which we from outside cannot begin to imagine. He has since been the object of admiration and compassion, but also of a variety of attempts to discredit and complicate a basically simple human fact: a man guilty of massive evil has been sorry and, in the hands of divine mercy, has redirected his life. Speer has been a transforming presence to other lives mangled by guilt, and he has been disbelieved and rejected.

I have never understood the importance of establishing whether or not Speer knew of the extermination program during his Hitler years. To blind oneself deliberately is a terrible thing. Complicity in evil because one has willfully destroyed one's capacity to recognize it (which is what he admitted, adding that had he known, he would have continued in Hitler's service) seems as wrong to me as complicity in an evil of which one has definite knowledge. The latter he denied.

Thin indeed is the line, if any, between repression and the deadening of our ability to see in the first place. The question, then, is not whether he knew originally more than he later realized, but whether conversion is possible to someone who is sorry for all he presently knows. It makes no theological sense to say no. He was telling the truth he knew, and the mystery of conversion is not so narrow that it refuses entrance to the fractured efforts of a wounded human psyche. If we can take more, we will be given more, but God does not fuss at the threshold.

The significant fact is not that Speer may have been worse than he could bear to remember, but that, when vomited onto the beach out of the belly of an unspeakable evil, he could go on living and so accept a vocation to a kind of prophecy of which he was to become his own word.

On the scales of repentance and atonement, he was a monumental figure on the basis of what he did know and admit. He was sorry for what he knew he knew, and that was a much greater load of guilt than most of us can carry.

So, having studied the evidence carefully, I'm not uncomfortable in accepting Albert Speer pretty much the way he presented himself, and as friends of his have assured me he was. Of course he was weak and vulnerable, of course he had human failings. That's what mercy is about. But I believe that he was real.

Is his account, even of what he knew, easier on himself than it might have been? Possibly, to some extent. Which of us could bear to be known — to ourselves or others — exactly as we are? A certain margin of this kind is always allowed in assessing autobiographical material. That does not lessen its essential truthfulness.

The Archetype

I was talking, at the beginning, about slums and death camps. Am I saying that they have simply to be forgiven, and everything will be all right? I hope I could not be so misunderstood. In the first place *they* are never to be forgiven. It is the repentant constructors of these earthly hells who are to be forgiven. And forgiveness is the landscape of conversion. I am saying that the response to mercy which we call conversion is the human way of dealing with horror and negation. And in this, Albert Speer is an incomparable instructor.

I have also said that here he is being used as an archetype; for this book is not a historical or biographical study, but an exploration of the spirit. He is here to be known, yes, but known as light on our own life's journey. Speer was a man who found God, himself, and the world in the mystery and miracle of forgiveness.

In the light of his experience, I believe we can encounter mercy, not as an unfortunate necessity of our flawed condition, but as an infinite form of reverence for our human dignity, as tender and adventurous: the other face of love.

"Lord if you had been here, my brother would not have died." There is more to the story than that. A dead man walked out of the tomb.

"Unbind him and set him free."

One day, some time in the summer of 1944, my friend Karl Hanke, the Gauleiter of Lower Silesia, came to see me. In earlier years he had told me a great deal about the Polish and French campaigns, had spoken of the dead and wounded, the pain and agonies, and in talking about these things had shown himself a man of sympathy and directness. This time, sitting in the green leather easy chair in my office, he seemed confused and spoke falteringly, with many breaks. He advised me never to accept an invitation to inspect a concentration camp in Upper Silesia. Never, under any circumstances. He had seen something there which he was not permitted to describe and moreover could not describe.

I did not query him, I did not query Himmler, I did not speak with personal friends. I did not investigate — for I did not want to know what was happening there. Hanke must have been speaking of Auschwitz. During those few seconds, while Hanke was warning me, the whole responsibility had become a reality again. Those seconds were uppermost in my mind when I stated to the international court at the Nuremberg Trial that as an important member of the leadership of the Reich, I had to share the total responsibility for all that had happened. For from that moment on, I was inescapably contaminated morally; from fear of discovering something which might have made me turn from my course, I had closed my eyes. This deliberate blindness outweighs whatever good I may have done or tried to do in the face of it. Because I failed at that time, I still feel, to this day, responsible for Auschwitz in a wholly personal sense.[1]

Part I

The Prisoner

Chapter 1

The Symbol

An American soldier in white helmet and white shoulder straps leads me down the basement corridors to a small elevator. Together, we ride up. A few steps down another corridor, a door opens, and I am standing on a small platform in the Nuremberg courtroom. A guard hands me earphones. In a daze, I hurry to put them on. Then I hear the judge's voice, sounding curiously impersonal and abstract through the mechanical medium: "Albert Speer, to twenty years imprisonment." I am aware of the eight judges looking down upon me, of the prosecutors, the defense attorneys, the correspondents, and spectators. But all that I really see are the dilated, shocked eyes of my lawyer, Dr. Hans Flächsner. Perhaps my heart stands still for a moment. Barely conscious of what I am doing. I bow silently to the judges. Then I am led through unfamiliar, dimly lit corridors to my cell. All this while the soldier to whom I am handcuffed has not said a word.[2]

Story

This is the story of a prisoner. It has grown a commentary because it asks questions — questions about the gift of life, its defilement, and the possibilities of reclamation. But it was a story before it was a meditation, and it will never cease to be a story, whatever else it has become as well.

Why story?

Because I'm convinced that human beings are story-telling

15

animals and God is a story-telling God, and that to outgrow the story is to outgrow our humanity.

It's hard to think of a more compelling description of the human condition than the story in which a man wrestles all night long and demands, with the dawn, a blessing as the price of letting his divine opponent go (Gen. 32:24–32).

When Jesus wanted to recommend kindness to us, he didn't say simply, "Be kind." He drew the verbal picture of a marginalized man who stopped to pick up and tend and shelter a mugging victim on the road to Jericho. And the Good Samaritan carried more than a dying man on his beast of burden. He comes to us still, bearing a load of theology and explaining salvation.

Story helps our hearts digest what our heads have taken in. The head is always quicker than the heart. The heart learns slowly; its knowledge struggles up out of life experience.

The heart needs story, which is truth with blood and nerves and history, with quarrels and meals and clothes — truth with a plot. The story can be an imaginative construct: tale, novel, drama. Or it can be a factual account. Each form in its own way can be as true as the other. Both have the goal of letting us live another life, and finding there both its meaning and our own. And so I like stories. They are truth I can get into, ache with, rejoice and grow with. They invite me into someone else's body and mind and emotional system, so that I need no longer be confined within my own.

The Symbol

But given all that, why the story of a prisoner? Some people know all about steel bars and guards and sentences. They are living the kind of life that comes to mind when the word "prison" is talked about. But not all of us are or have been that kind of prisoner. So how universal is the story I am going to use as the framework of this book, and how many of us can be reached by the life of Albert Speer, who spent twenty years confined to an antiquated prison on the outskirts of Berlin because he had been a leader in one of the most barbarous political regimes the world has known?

How universal indeed.

In one of the great "O Antiphons" of the Advent season, we ask the Key of David to let us out of prison. The liturgy knows, of course, that all of us aren't locked into cell blocks. But it also knows there are prisons and prisons. The cell and the bars are a telling symbol with a long literary and spiritual history. Remember the cold, wretched trek from Moscow in which Tolstoy's Pierre finally discovers his dignity and the meaning of his life? "It's as if he had just come out of a Russian bath; do you understand? Out of a moral bath." Natasha says.[3] Remember the multitude of variously imprisoned characters who people Dickens's *Little Dorrit,* and spend the whole long story getting out of, getting into, or remaining stuck in their individual forms of imprisonment?

It's not the most comfortable image in the world, but as we follow it through the twenty years of Speer's life in Spandau, we can watch it expanding into one symbol after another, offering us both comfort and challenge. We are not too good for it; and it need not be morbid or depressing. It can be an image of hope.

I don't know exactly what led me to Speer's memoirs, or what they were even doing in our library. I do know that in them, and in his prison diaries, I found a storied description of the human heart in God's redemptive embrace. I have come to a new understanding of forgiveness, because I have seen it at work in this man's life.

I have not chosen the story of a perfect man. After all, this is an exploration of forgiveness, and mercy neither asks nor makes perfection. That's the trouble. We'd be a whole lot more comfortable if we had only to push a few buttons, mount a determined effort at self-improvement, and walk out — perfect or at least generally unobjectionable — from the redemptive mechanism.

Redemption doesn't work that way, and so this is the story of someone more gifted than most, but flawed and vulnerable, a stone of scandal to some, but caught up in the inexplicable dynamism of God's mercy. This is the story of someone deeply human, someone God loved above all calculation.

And because I believe in a God for whom no man is an island, I believe that Albert Speer's life is not his alone. He is not an isolated individual with a remarkable vocation. He is you and me; and that is why these reflections move back and forth between his life and ours. They are not so much a study of his life as a meditation on the identification of his life and ours, his story and ours. For though our lives may be less dramatic, they are no less redeemed.

Chapter 2

The Prisoner

More than twenty thousand pages lay before me when I opened the trunk in which my family had stored all the writings that I had sent to them from Nuremberg and Spandau in the course of more than twenty years....

If I read the whole thing rightly, these thousands of notes are one concentrated effort to survive, an endeavor not only to endure life in a cell physically and intellectually, but also to arrive at some sort of moral reckoning with what lay behind it all....

For many years after midnight on September 30, 1966, when the gates of Spandau opened for me, I shied away from looking at that mass of papers which is all that has remained of my life between my fortieth and my sixtieth years. There are various reasons for my presenting this journal now. But ultimately it is an attempt to give form to the time that seemed to be pouring away so meaninglessly, to give substance to years empty of content. Diaries are usually the accompaniment of a lived life. This one stands in place of a life.[4]

Does it?

Perhaps the answer depends on what one considers a life. To me, for whom Albert Speer is a revelation of what human life is all about, these years were far from meaningless. I am honestly convinced that there was more life going on in that small prison cell, in the corridor that he swept and the garden he created, than in our government offices, university classrooms, research centers, industrial complexes, and — a great deal of the time — our churches.

What was he doing there? He hadn't come because he wanted to; in fact, he'd have given anything to unmake the career which had led to Spandau.

On the evening of... May 1, when Hitler's death was announced, I slept in a small room in Doenitz's quarters. When I unpacked my bag I found the red leather case containing Hitler's portrait. My secretary had included it in my luggage. My nerves had reached their limit. When I stood the photograph up, a fit of weeping overcame me. That was the end of my relationship to Hitler. Only now was the spell broken, the magic extinguished. What remained were images of graveyards, of shattered cities, of millions of mourners, of concentration camps. Not all these images came into my mind at this moment, but they were there, somehow present in me. I fell into a deep, exhausted sleep.

Two weeks later, staggered by the revelations of the crimes in the concentration camps, I wrote to the chairman of the ministerial cabinet, Scherwin-Krosigk: "The previous leadership of the German nation bears a collective guilt for the fate that now hangs over the German people. Each member of that leadership must personally assume his responsibility in such a way that the guilt which might otherwise descend upon the German people is expiated."

With that, there began a segment of my life which has not ended to this day.[5]

On July 19, 1947, seven members of Hitler's high command were transported to Spandau Prison from the trial prison at Nuremberg. Walter Funk had been Minister of Economics in the Third Reich. Rudolf Hess had been Hitler's deputy, Constantin von Neurath his foreign minister at the beginning of the war. Baldur von Shirach, leader of the Hitler Youth, had, as he put it, "taught the youth of Germany to worship the murderer of millions." All four had taken conspicuous roles in Hitler's attempt to exterminate the Jews. Grand Admiral Erich Raeder and Grand Admiral Karl Doenitz had served in turn as commanders of the German navy, and Doenitz had succeeded Hitler just in time to surrender to the Allies. The seventh prisoner was Albert Speer.

Of the other Nuremberg defendants, two had been acquitted, and Goering had committed suicide after being sentenced. Eleven had been hanged; for them the war and its consequences ended on October 16, 1946; not for Speer.

Perhaps the way these men have ended their lives is preferable to my situation; that is the thought that comes to me this morning. When I spoke to Dr. Pflucker a few days ago about the fear felt by the men awaiting death, he told me he had permission to give them all a strong sedative before the execution. Now the thought of that fills me with something akin to envy: it's all over for them. I still have to face twenty years. Will I live through them? Yesterday I tried to imagine myself leaving prison after two decades, an old man.[6]

The Architect

"Yes, the architect," murmured an official to whom the prisoners were being shown, rather like animals in a zoo. Yes, the architect. Speer had followed his father into the profession, and had made no startling success of it, when a haphazard collection of circumstance, coincidence, and unreflective choice delivered his twenty-eight-year-old talent to Adolf Hitler. Had circumstance been content with dropping him there, he would have ended as a historical footnote: Hitler's court architect, the drawer of plans and the maker of mock-ups never to be built, the designer of a megalomaniacal dreamworld. He would have read about Spandau in the news and gone about his business, making money and taking creative pleasure in the rebuilding of postwar Germany.

However, on February 9, 1942, Dr. Fritz Todt was killed in a plane crash, by accident or design. Hitler chose Speer, his favored protégé, to replace him as Minister of Armaments and War Production. Albert Speer had never used a military weapon, knew nothing of armaments, and, except for his construction contacts, had no industrial experience. Yet, like a sleepwalker, as he later said, he walked unerringly from one decision to another. His genius was adaptable. The accomplishment of this task absorbed his mind; its consequences did not.

Conviction

He was not convicted of war crimes because he had produced arms, or because his remarkable management had prolonged the war. The legal basis for his conviction lay in the deportation of forced labor from occupied countries for the purpose of armament production. World War II statistics are understandably unreliable, but we know that at least 7.5 million deportees worked in German industry during the war.

> *The necessary labor force...was to come from the occupied territories. Hitler instructed Sauckel to bring the needed workers in by any means whatsoever. That order marked the beginning of a fateful segment of my work.... I helped Sauckel gain authority and helped him wherever I could.*[7]

It is not known how many of these were alive to return to their homes after the war, or how many had homes to go to. The Nuremberg convictions were based on four counts: plotting a war of aggression; prosecution of such a war; war crimes; and crimes against humanity. Speer was convicted on the latter two counts. His sentence was mitigated from death or life imprisonment because the Western judges took into account extenuating circumstances: the more humane conditions of factory workers under his jurisdiction, and his final opposition to Hitler, carried out in extremely dangerous circumstances.

But though the court assessed his guilt in terms of the Geneva Convention, the legal sentence was not the only — or even the most important — reason for Speer's imprisonment. He himself realized that the moral issue far outweighed the legal, and that as a leader, his own responsibility extended beyond the violation of his workers' rights into the whole of Hitler's crimes. Too late had he acknowledged the nature of the regime and the character of the conflict his genius was sustaining. He testified at Nuremberg and continued to maintain that he had known too late of the atrocities, too late confronted the inevitability of generations warped and tormented by the war he had served and prolonged. Too late he counted deaths that should never have been. He had not known, because he had not wanted to know.

Chapter 3

Forgiveness: The Difficulty

> But O thou tyrant!
> Do not repent these things, for they are heavier
> Than all thy woes can stir; therefore betake thee
> To nothing but despair. A thousand knees
> Ten thousand years together, naked, fasting,
> Upon a barren mountain, and still winter
> In storm perpetual, could not move the gods
> To look that way thou wert.
>
> —Shakespeare, *The Winter's Tale*, III, 2

So does Paulina curse Leontes in *The Winter's Tale*. Shakespeare has created some splendid cursing women, and at times we might well feel like looking up their lines just to satisfy our frustrated longing for moral order in the face of mass graves, contemporary slave trading, systematic rape, and swarms of children making sewers into home. To eyes swimming with horror, forgiveness can take on the appearance of betrayal. To forgive — is it not abandonment of the victimized, collusion in atrocity?

This is the chapter in which I want to listen to the people who can't forgive, people who are convinced that evil of a certain dimension can never be forgiven. For their words are many-layered. They are saying something important about themselves and God and human relations. Moral conviction can feel genuinely obliged to qualify the promises of Isaiah's God: "If their sins be like scarlet, I will make them white as wool." Although I don't agree with them, I run the risk of cheapening the reality of forgiveness and erasing its mystery if I fail to take their reluctances seriously. Mercy is not a facile solution to anyone's moral perplexity.

More than this, the difficulty of forgiving can have deeply tangled roots. Human history is no stranger to vengeance, as it is no stranger to violence. Even vengeance, which in seeking to redress disorder only succeeds in perpetuating the cycle of violence, can be seen as the distortion of something good. It is a misguided form of asserting our radical need for order and stability. Vengeance imposes a primitive form of justice on a situation which threatens to consume our world in unresisted force.

We need to know that evil has a name, and that its agents are taking up at least some of the painful consequences of destructive action and intent. As deceptive as it is, a spirit of reprisal can mitigate the fear of meaninglessness. We ought to know better, but we continue to feel that getting back at "them" somehow makes up for the damage they have done and can prevent it from happening again.

How We Feel about It

A further factor in our troubles with forgiveness is pure pain. Those who have been so radically afflicted that they deny the possibility of healing or forgiveness, and those who have so deeply hurt another that they deny the possibility of being forgiven, have gained considerable knowledge of the mystery of forgiveness, but can find themselves lost in what seems to be the pathless woods of suffering.

We can earnestly want bad people to stay bad. We would prefer them to forestall mercy by a refusal of remorse. Let them not be converted lest they escape the punishment we'd like to see them get. There's understandable emotion here, together with an insistence on justice. Pain twists the brain as well as the heart.

Or we may want to make them out as evil as we can, for sometimes we want to gain the greatest distance from someone else's guilt, and in Speer's case, from the moral climate of Nazi

Germany. But what's wrong with admitting, "I could have done that too"? The rest of us are beneficiaries of a Providence that protected people like us, who are too weak, from having to take the road of such radical repentance.

On April 9, 1888, a fifteen-year-old girl from an extremely sheltered home entered an enclosed monastery in France; she died at twenty-four. She had no trouble identifying with the guilt of humanity, and knew that only God's preventive grace had saved her from actions as monstrous as Speer's. Her memoirs begin with a text from Psalm 88: "The mercies of the Lord I will sing forever." What on earth had she done, this daughter of a narrow bourgeois family? Nothing much; she hadn't had the opportunity. Yet her theological insight into the redemptive solidarity of the world was immense and rocklike. Thérèse Martin knew. She could not have dissociated herself from Albert Speer without annihilating the meaning and purpose of her life.

The Reasons

I have reasons for pausing on the difficulties of mercy. One reason is simply that the mercy we're talking about has to be the real thing — the exalted, hard, and shocking thing it really is. It has to be God's lavish, eruptive, passionate embrace, and not the dusty provincial virtue we have assumed we know all about. In facing and trying to absorb the fury directed against Albert Speer, I have come myself to understand redemption in a way I never did before. Unless we've measured the scandalous breadth of mercy, how can we know God? And what can we know about that Jesus whom the Creed confesses?

The Unforgiven?

Another reason is an attempt to grasp the several perspectives from which Speer has come to be viewed. We have seen that for many observers he is unforgivable and unforgiven, a man who can't be credited with any moral sense. To court for him the possibility of mercy is fruitless and obscene. The parable of the

Lost Sheep does not apply when the sheep is Hitler's right-hand man. This is understandable, though it confuses irretrievably the action and the man — as if granting mercy to Speer were the equivalent of approving the death camps; as if the only way of repudiating Belsen were to deny the possibility of remorse and renewal to an individual responsible for its existence.

Or can it be true that when we can't reverse the consequences of our evil choices, God has no way of re-creating the world we have destroyed, and so cannot forgive? But how many of the consequences in an ordinary life can be reversed? On how many of our self-centered and stumbling refusals to be human and mature can we turn back the clock? Refuse forgiveness? In what coils of despair would then our tortured logic bind us forever.

It's only the dimensions of evil then? Only the degree of the crime, the number of its victims, the intensity of the pain? That doesn't work either. The logic must hold. If irreversible consequences prevent the offering of mercy, then we are all sunk. There is no margin for sin, and the whole idea of forgiveness has to be erased from human expectation. Who would draw the line: this much can be atoned for, and beyond...?

When Corrie Ten Boom left Ravensbruk, she went out to preach forgiveness, and who can accuse her of thereby minimizing the suffering of the Jews for whose sake she had suffered imprisonment?

The Guilt of Repression

Conversion has many forms. If it *were* true that Speer had lacked the courage to face repressed knowledge, this would only mean that he had not been taught, or had not been able to grasp, the full nature of mercy and its totally renewing power. Remorse is only the beginning of conversion, not its full scope. And if all we're given by way of instruction in the divine mercy is the necessity for remorse, restitution, and expiation, naturally we'll be terrified of facing the fullness of the monster we are afraid we really are. We have to know conversion as something so vast that no extremity of guilt can stand against its jubilant incoming tides. We have to know that the one who enjoys the privileged place in the heart of God is the one who offers to divine mercy the most to forgive.

But if we don't recognize the fullness of redemption, we are not thereby inadequately redeemed. It may be the other way around. Our anguished fear of having been too guilty to be forgiven may haunt our lives and weld us even more closely to the abandoned Christ who "became sin" for our sakes, and whose redemptive offering we have so deeply entered.

To Be Shocked

I've said that many of us have no trouble identifying with Speer's journey: monastics, for instance. One of the gifts of monastic living is a sense of solidarity with the weak and wounded. This is a gift shared by many other of the people who have read his books with relief and joy. It is this journey, into mercy and beyond, that I would like to share with you. I would like you to walk up to this mercy as if you'd never known it, challenge it, and find that, wonderfully, it holds.

Ask of it whether, in the forgiveness of this man, it is ignoring our need for order, retribution, and the reconstruction of chaos. Are we being left parched for meaning on a shale of irresponsible choices?

All the accusations are legitimate, except... except they are not true. Surrender to the gift of mercy has to involve acknowledgment of moral order and the return to it. In the desert legends of the harlot who dies immediately of mercy's very joy, the return is instant and ecstatic. In Speer's also, the forgiveness is immediate, though the remaking of his soul has to be measured in years; and even then, perhaps it won't please everyone. God has strange taste in heroes. But whatever the form of our acceptance, God's vengeance lies in our conversion. To say this, and to say it with great conviction, is not to dilute the mystery.

Albert Speer was a Christian; so am I, and so I will have to talk about his spiritual journey in a Christian context. But no one, not I certainly, nor anyone else, can make that journey completely understandable. World War II is not understandable to begin with, and neither is Hitler. It's no secret that the human situation in general proves itself murky and unsatisfactory to the orderly mind. Our commonest forms of guilt and heroism are mysterious enough. How much less penetrable has to be the encounter of such an immense evil with a mercy even greater, of such guilt with redemption.

> But God, who is rich in mercy, out of the great love with which he loved us even when we were dead through our trespasses, made us alive together with Christ... so that in the ages to come, he might show the immeasurable riches of his grace in kindness toward us in Christ Jesus.
>
> (Eph. 2:4–7 NRSV)

I respect the voice that refuses mercy in the name of justice and order. They say that if a man like Speer can be sorry and find mercy, the world must stand without redress. But I say that if a man like Speer cannot find sorrow and forgiveness, the world is truly lost and without succor.

And so we have a man quite simply doing what he can. For twenty years, in what might be called a quasi-monastic commitment, his sense of guilt would face the world he had so unspeakably damaged, but also the God of whose immeasurable mercy the prophet had sung. Immeasurable, yes, but not simple; for though God is simple, the human heart is not.

Chapter 4

The Icon

Albert Speer was not forced into a career of destruction. Yet we find at the outset of his career several strokes of luck at which we want desperately to call, "Lord, if you had been there...." Hitler would have done so much less damage if someone had derailed the idealistic young man who dropped in on the Nazi party after one of his speeches. Yet no hand reached out to disable the mechanisms by which he emerged at Hitler's side. Is this a good case for the prosecution of the inert God? For God stood by, as it were, and let be. But I believe that his letting-be was — scandalously, dreadfully — an expression of love. God loved this man enough to let him walk, self-blinded and alone, into a place of unimaginable darkness, to become the intimate of the twin accusations we are so fond of throwing in the face of God: evil and suffering.

Do not ask me why God permitted Hitler. I do not believe in a helpless or inert God. I do believe in a God who respects human choice enough to let it take disastrous initiatives. God can afford to put himself one-down, to hold back his own hand and operate in a negation of our ideologies of power and control, because in the wreckage he permits us to make of his world, God has placed a dynamism which saves, upholds, and re-creates. Buchenwald does not have the last word.

Believing this does not erase the mystery. If it did, it would erase God. Someday, after our mortal lives have been swallowed up in immortality, we will know more about it — but never all. The difference will lie in this: that then the mystery which here weighs and oppresses will have become instead a source of delight and peace.

However, it is not Hitler I am reflecting on. Given Hitler, given the war, why did no hand move, when such a slight movement would have saved Speer from so unspeakable a destiny? And I am daring to say that there was greater love in the folded hands than there would have been in the preventive touch.

A vocation is as mysterious as the God who calls and as complex as the world to which this calling is meant to minister. If a certain boat trip had begun an hour earlier, or Speer's life had begun a few years later, or Todt's plane had not crashed, or Hitler had not fancied himself an architect and so projected onto this young man his own fantasies and ambitions...then, yes, Speer would have assisted profitably in the material rebirth of Germany and never known Spandau.

And the weaknesses which led to his position in Hitler's dismal entourage would have created for him instead a respectable, constructive life. His moral weakness would have kept him moral. A prosperous, creative architect with plenty of scope for his ego, he would have found no advantage in reaching beyond the conventions of morality; they would have been profitable to him. He would have been satisfied, and he would have been warned. Rubble and death are effective roadblocks to ambitions based on conquest, and there would have been no temptation of this sort to withstand.

Yet God did not reach out to shield Speer from himself. God did not even shield the world from the perversion of this man's extensive gifts. He was born when he was born, and he allowed himself to be swept into the orbit of the man of whom he was to say at Nuremberg: "If Hitler had ever had a friend, I would have been his close friend."

The point is not that this happened, much less that its happening was divinely ordained and inescapable (which is certainly not true), but that in not withdrawing from Speer's weaknesses the catalyst that would activate them, God was entrusting him with a particularly ravaging vocation. His own moral disintegration would spare him from material success and deliver him over to the redeeming power of a great love.

What's wrong with respectability? Nothing at all. Morality is a fine thing. But there are respectable lives which say little of love and nothing of forgiveness. We certainly could have done without World War II, which was, after all, the choice of men and not of God. But given World War II, we needed the story of Speer and of the immense moral courage with which he allowed God to remake his life. God was lover and destiny for Speer. He would not let him settle for less.

The Ministry

A personal destiny is not the only element of a vocation, nor was it in the call of Albert Speer. He was asked, for our sakes, to let himself become an icon of redemption.

If we find it difficult to see him as an image of redeemed humanity, we can try saying the Creed and hear, perhaps for the first time, "I believe in the forgiveness of sins." I believe, I really do. It's possible.

But then to take the other step and stand before the full exuberance of divine mercy is to see him, not as a second-class citizen of the Kingdom, but an image of Christ the Redeemer, in fact a member of his body and a participant in his saving work. How can this be?

How can this partial and limited atonement for his own immeasurable sin reach beyond his own guilt and touch that of the world with healing and grace? How can I call this man a Christ figure?

For one thing, because we are all Christ figures.

Since human nature as He assumed it was not annulled, by that very fact it has been raised up to a divine dignity in our respect too. For by His incarnation the Son of God has united Himself in some fashion with every man. He worked with human hands, He thought with a human mind, acted by human choice, and loved with a human heart. Born of the Virgin Mary, He has truly been made one of us, like us in all things except sin.[8]

In addition, Speer's atonement was not measured solely by itself. His own atonement was the little he could contribute to an absolute reparation pressed into his hands in the first broken moment of repentance. When he walked into Spandau, Speer was a man absolved, a man made innocent and given his share in the mediation of Christ, whose perfect atonement and reparative power had become his own. Here was a strange and strangely beautiful figure of innocence.

Mercy itself, as a perfection of the infinite God, is also infinite. Also infinite therefore and inexhaustible is the Father's readiness to receive the prodigal children who return to his home. Infinite are the readiness and power of forgiveness which flow continually from the marvelous value of the sacrifice of the Son. No human sin can prevail over this power or even limit it. On the part of man, only a lack of good will can limit it, a lack of readiness to be converted and to repent.[9]

Speer's repentance had plunged him into the redeeming Christ, and through his human choices and acts flowed the reparative sacrifice of the Son of God. We take this bit of theology for granted, don't we, until the wrong to be forgiven is monumental, until we encounter it, living and sublime, in the life of a human being to whom some of us may hesitate to extend our own forgiveness.

Reconstruction

But was the Speer of the Nuremberg Trial the same man who left Spandau in a storm of flashbulbs on September 30, 1966? Hardly. Forgiveness is a complex business. As he enters the gates of Spandau, he is carrying his objective innocence in a personality still wounded and confused by early emotional deprivation and the destructive choices of his life. He has a long way to go, but not alone. Spandau had a purpose, to Speer himself and to the world. In giving himself to the work of personal reconstruction, he was carrying a wounded world into the heart of God. In giving his own moral wounds to be healed, wounds acquired through embracing the destructive values of his world, he was helping to cleanse that world, in Christ, of the damage wrought by those values. Conversion works this way for all of us. It is not a work of isolation. In our personal remaking, our world comes with us, "for we, who are many, are one body in Christ, and individually we are members one of another," and "must grow up in every way into him who is the head, into Christ...from whom the whole body, joined and knit together by every ligament with which it is equipped, as each part is working properly, promotes the body's growth in building itself up in love" (Rom. 12:5; Eph. 4:15–16 NRSV).

His was the terrible vocation of recognizing the evil into which he had allowed himself to be drawn, and of immersing this responsibility in the saving death of Christ. In silence and solitude, poverty and stability, his own transformation was helping to transform the world.

The Human Vocation

Well, yes. But after all, very few of us have assisted at the gas chambers and crematoria of the world. We do our best. What in this man is so universal? Why does he express so clearly the human vocation?

I suppose we might ask first, What *is* the human vocation? "What are you here for?" is a question that acts like sandpaper on my capacity for reaction. It has its variants, of course. It can be, "What did you expect when you got married?" Or "What are we all doing on this murderous planet?" Or for people like me, "Why did you enter a monastery?"

The trouble with it is its unexpressed overtones: "Well, you wanted to change the world. You wanted to achieve some great moral excellence. You had ideas about self-oblation and cheerful penance. Well, get at it." My married friends can hear in it, "Remember how you looked forward to years of consecrated intimacy, to rearing a family for Christ, and contributing to a new and constructive generation. You must have done something wrong along the way. Your life would hardly look so bruised and ordinary had you put a little more effort into the project."

"Get with it," this inner accusation continues. "Why are you dodging down those little back alleys of comfort? Why do you carry such a burden of complaint and bear so reluctantly the uncongenial task? Why is it always someone else's fault, and how come you cling like a tick to some job or piece of status that plumps your ego? Go on back to the vision you had at the beginning and make it real." Just like that. Just by determining.

But the question doesn't have to have such a negative over-load.

It's a beautiful question. What it really means is: "Why were you so carefully crafted, so lovingly made? Why was life placed in your hands at all, and where are you meant to carry it?" These are the questions we could stop on. They aren't yellowed and dog-eared. They're fresh and life-giving. They're what make the life of Albert Speer a place to stop and wonder in, a place to worship in, a place to learn about ourselves, and share, somehow, his mission and his transformation. Where are we supposed to carry this gift?

What are we after all?

There are many ways of saying it, of saying the one thing we spend our lives rediscovering, we time-bound children of eternity, we who are to ourselves the question only God can answer.[10]

We are they who are made to gaze at a beauty that transcends our power of sight, and to survive the view; to be upheld and protected by the shattering embrace of eternal love; to find we are more than ourselves in the celebration of our limitations and our dignity.

We are they who are meant to stand at the summit of creation, in communion with all that has being, linking the divine and the material in our own stammerings of praise.

And the interesting thing is that all this incredible stuff has to be worked out in the context of redemption. We are not simply loved; we are saved. We are not simply made for eternity; we are being remade every moment of our lives. Toward us, divine love turns the face we call mercy, the mercy which draws good from all the forms of evil existing in the world and in us.[11]

And this is where the image of imprisonment comes in handy.

For we are all truly imprisoned, and if we're the least bit smart we know it — in sin and guilt, in our emotional disabilities and disordered coping mechanisms, in our perfectly good and admirable natural limitations, in our personal history and the history of our race, in our cultural and family heritage.

It's important to realize how much of this is good. But obviously not all of it is. We have ample evidence for this, in our own lives and in the papers.

Guilt

Guilt: what is it? Is it real? Sometimes. Speer's was. It isn't always so, of course, for there is guilt and guilt. There is the acting out of some evil intent, or the deliberate refusal to recognize that what one is doing is wrong. That's the real thing. Then there's the uncertainty of whether, given precise circumstances, the precise degree of pressure, we might well choose the evil ourselves, choose not to see and speak. This is why studies of Nazi Germany always make me nervous. Would I have seen and spoken? Would I have given myself for my Jewish brother or sister, or would I have chosen to know nothing and to get on with my life?

I was not tested like that. My own opportunities for self-interested choices are mundane and petty. But with the advantages I have, can my acts of moral cowardice be dismissed as minor eccentricities?

Do we consider often enough that guilt is not measured by the extent of the damage one has done? Someone with a restricted scope for consequences may have a far more extensively diseased moral constitution than Speer's. This is not a defense. It is only an attempt to demonstrate our identification with this man who offered himself in all honesty to a redemption we all need.

...We all need. Don't we also recognize the experience of feeling that the evil of the entire world has been tipped out over our head and is flowing into the marrow of our bones? It's more than "I am no better than they," or "There but for the grace of God...." It's "I *am* they." We can certainly feel as if we are, and Jesus probably did too on the bloody grass of Gethsemani. In some way, he "became sin, who knew no sin." And we?

But say that my sense of guilt is a vague, global discomfort. I have been conditioned to feel awful about myself, and this is part of that package. It's important for our mental health to distinguish real from unreal guilt. But when we consider forgiveness, as we will, when we consider the prison experience, we need not distinguish too finely. Forgiveness embraces every form of guilt, even the kind which is not guilt at all, but only the sense which somebody left with us when we were small of being no good, the sense of never doing anything right. Sometimes when we can't talk ourselves into feeling wonderful about ourselves, we need to know we are forgiven just for being who we are. And however wild and unhealthy that is, it's still nice to know such mercy is available.

Chapter 5

The Builder

The Berlin Chancellery, Speer's single great completed building, had been finished:

> Forty-five hundred workers had labored in two shifts to meet the deadline.... The whole work force, masons, carpenters, plumbers, and so on, were invited to inspect the building and filed awestruck through the finished rooms. Hitler addressed them in the Sportpalast:
> "I stand here as representative of the German people. And whenever I receive anyone in the Chancellery, it is not the private individual Adolf Hitler who receives him, but the leader of the German nation — and therefore it is not I who receive him but Germany through me. For that reason I want these rooms to be in keeping with their high mission. Every individual has contributed to a structure that will outlast the centuries and will speak to posterity of our times. This is the first architectural creation of the new, great German Reich!"[12]

All right, God let be. But from what was he holding back his hand? What pulled this intelligent and cultured man into the orbit of such a dark star? With the possible exceptions of Goebbels, with his high talent for reconstituting reality, and Goering, whose potential lost itself in drugs, Hitler's associates were a collection of mediocrities. Morality was not the only area in which they were unimpressive.

Speer, instead, was gifted, the brilliant sort of man who can, unfortunately, do what he sets out to do. The young Speer was handsome, impressionable, quiet, fiercely concentrated. Emotionally deprived as a child, he was reserved rather than cold, with a capacity for phenomenal calm. He was to be envied, fought, and disliked as distant and more efficient than human. He was to gain loyalty, affection, and respect — in some cases, adoration. This was part of the trouble, as he reflects when told of the respect in which the Western judges had held him in Nuremberg:

> *I recall my teacher Tessenow, who so conspicuously gave me his backing when I was a student, and then Hitler, and then these judges, and now many of the guards. It is an advantage to be liked, but to think it nothing but an advantage is being very simplistic indeed. Perhaps in a way it is my life's problem.... Someday I must try to work this one out completely.[13]*

And then Hitler.

It's hard for us to conceive of Hitler as personally attractive. He must have been tremendously so, but we take it on trust. Particularly hard to understand is how he could lay a spell of any permanence on those who knew him well. According to Speer's description, he must have been an awful bore. And yet the two men were deeply bonded by a complex of emotion that Speer himself, much less Hitler, probably never fully understood.

Years after the death of Hitler, he reflects,

> *Hitler. Suddenly he has again become present to my mind. I had almost driven him from my thoughts. How long it is since I have written about him. Almost nothing for years, I imagine, aside from anecdotes and an odd remark here and there.... If I look searchingly into myself, I must say that this is scarcely due to my having rid myself of him. Rather, it seems to me that I have been evading him because he still has too strong a hold on me. Whatever turn my life takes in the future, whenever my name is mentioned, people will think of Hitler. I shall never have an independent existence. And sometimes I see myself as*

*a man of seventy, children long since adult and grand-
children growing up, and wherever I go people will not
ask about me but about Hitler.*[14]

I am not ready to psychoanalyze the attraction, or beyond
a very simple point, the man. For my purposes, I do not need
to. The bond was there; that is enough to know. It was there
for others also, but for none who had so close a view of the
Fuehrer, or for whom the opportunity for disillusion was so
great. That he continuously chose to refuse this opportunity
created the tragedy of his life.

A Second Schinkel

Easier to assess is the force of Hitler's appeal to raw ambition.
More than the position of favored protégé to a world leader,
more than a personal devotion to Hitler himself, Speer wanted
success. And here was the deadly combination: a high degree of
dependence and an immense passion for fame, both centered on
the same man, Adolf Hitler.

*Tonight I have done a bit of arithmetic. I was twenty-six
when I first heard Hitler speak — up to then he had not
interested me at all. I was thirty when he laid a world
at my feet. I did not help him to power, did not finance
his rearmament. My dreams always were concerned with
buildings; it was not power I wanted, but to become a
second Schinkel.*[15]

Karl Friedrich Schinkel was the great architect with whose
buildings Speer was living in the Berlin of his day.

*For a commission to do a great building, I would have
sold my soul like Faust's. Now I had found my Mephi-
stopheles.*[16]

This is a retrospective remark, of course, for at the time, he
did not recognize the satanic element in his patron. All was
opportunity.

During the twenty years I spent in Spandau prison I often asked myself what I would have done if I had recognized Hitler's real face and the true nature of the regime he had established. The answer was banal and dispiriting: my position as Hitler's architect had soon become indispensable to me. Not yet thirty, I saw before me the most exciting prospects an architect can dream of.[17]

Albert Speer was not a bad man. This is the frightening part of his story. He had no desire to conquer the world, no interest in military glory, and no spirit of anti-Semitism. He simply longed to ascend into "the heaven of history," to produce "a body of work that would place me among the outstanding architects of history." We look today at plans and models of a demoniacally outsized cityscape, and shiver at an intelligence so childishly degraded. "Demonic" is, by the way, an accurate term, for he saw clearly how Hitler's distorted religious sense was calling upon his architect to create a material setting for the rites of Fuehrer worship. (This created problems in itself: the vast size of Hitler's Great Hall would have reduced its object of worship to the size of a fly on the wall; fortunately this was a problem that went up in the fires of a defeated Berlin.)

"Childish" is also a descriptively appropriate word. We can often see through games of glory to the incomplete personalities playing beneath. In one form or another, they strut or cry, manipulate or build in a desperate bid for attention. The attention may be world class, but the games betray their nursery origin. Hitler shows his kinship with the schoolyard bully; Speer betrays the expansive daydreams of the very young, and we — do we see through our own respectable ploys?

So Speer was homesick for glory, and his own compulsions built for him a prison of ambition. When called from his architectural interests to a cabinet position, he was able to transfer a technician's obsession with the exercise of a mechanical craft to the running of a successful munitions industry. He didn't really like the job and had no special interest in the war it was prolonging, except as substance for the exaltation of the man he planned to immortalize. It was a task to be run, a mechanical and organizational project to be undertaken for the sheer accomplishment of the technical challenge.

> For me personally, the great change did not take place until Feb. 8, 1942. As Hitler's architect, nothing would have happened to me after a lost war; I would not even have been called up before the German denazification authorities.... No one would have brought an architect to trial. My associates who worked with me on the plans for Berlin are back at work today, so my wife writes; they are doing well as city planners and architects and are even able to help out my family.[18]

> Hitler received me officially as Fuehrer of the Reich.... "Herr Speer, I appoint you the successor to Minister Todt in all his capacities...in all his capacities, including Minister of Armaments."[19]

> One can only wonder at the recklessness and frivolity with which Hitler appointed me to one of those three or four ministries on which the existence of the state depended. I was a complete outsider to the army, to the party, and to industry. Never in my life had I had anything to do with military weapons.[20]

Can we really believe he had not angled for the job, that, like a few other fortuitous moments in his career, this one too simply fell into his lap? We know that his place in Hitler's favor was not the product of circumstance alone. He furthered his advantages; he fought for much of what he, unfortunately, got. But when he calls the armaments ministry unwanted and unsought, I believe him. It would take more than supposition to convince me otherwise. He was an artist; that was his area of ambition. And when reading his account of life in the armaments ministry, you wonder how he could have survived ten days of it, let alone made of it the success that he did.

At a Price

Success as a minister, as success in architecture, came at a price. Even before his appointment to the ministry he had been a workaholic. Now he became even more radically prisoner of the mechanical, the organizational. Addiction to work is true addiction, and with the addict's tunnel vision, Speer poured his entire self — his body with its skills, his cultured mind, his time and energy and capacity for interest — into the narrow channel of an obsessive work pattern, interrupted only when he was compelled to waste an amount of his time on personal presence to Hitler. Naturally, he had long ceased to be any kind of presence to his family.

> *I gave up the real center of my life: my family. Completely under the sway of Hitler, I was henceforth possessed by my work. Nothing else mattered.*[21]

> *My family lived happily in this house. I wish I could write that I had a share in this familial happiness, as my wife and I had once dreamed. But by the time I arrived home, it would be late in the evening and the children would have long since been put to bed. I would sit with my wife for a while — silent from exhaustion. This kind of rigidity became more and more the norm, and when I consider the matter in retrospect, what was happening to me was no different from what was happening to the party bigwigs, who ruined their family life by their ostentatious style of living. They froze into poses of officialism. My own rigidity sprang from excessive work.*[22]

But probably the most destructive effect of preoccupation with his career was a steadily increasing blindness to the values he was absorbing. Unable or unwilling to acknowledge the essential nature of the regime, he was even less aware of what was happening within himself.

> *An American historian has said of me that I loved machines more than people. He is not wrong.*[23]

This is obvious in Speer's third book, *The Infiltrator*, which though unfaithful to his talents as a writer, provides a stifling account of the world which was transforming his humanity into a machine.

Even in his architectural days, he had not seen that his cultural and architectural values were eroding under his feet.

> [*The design for Goering's headquarters*] *was a decisive step in my personal development from the neoclassicism I had first espoused...to a blatant* nouveau riche *architecture of prestige.*[24]

The Question

Most terribly, he did not realize how radically he had lost the human and moral standards he had taken for granted.

> *On November 10, driving to the office, I passed by the still smoldering ruins of the Berlin synagogues....Today that memory is one of the most doleful of my life....I did not see that more was being smashed than glass, that on that night Hitler had crossed a Rubicon,...had taken a step that irrevocably sealed the fate of his country. Did I sense, at least for a moment, that something was beginning which would end with the annihilation of one whole group of our nation? Did I sense that this outburst of hoodlumism was changing my moral substance? I do not know.*
>
> *During the years after my release from Spandau I have been repeatedly asked what thoughts I had on this subject during my two decades alone in the cell with myself; what I actually knew of the persecution, the deportation, and the annihilation of the Jews; what I should have known and what conclusions I ought to have drawn.*
>
> *I no longer give the answers with which I tried for so long to soothe the questioners, but chiefly myself...for they are efforts at legalistic exculpation. It is true that*

...I was isolated. It is also true that the habit of thinking within the limits of my own field provided me...with many opportunities for evasion. It is true that I did not know what was really beginning on Nov 9, 1938, and what ended in Auschwitz and Maidanek. But in the final analysis I myself determined the degree of my isolation, the extremity of my evasions, and the extent of my ignorance.

I therefore know today that my agonized self-examinations posed the question as wrongly as did the questioners whom I have met since my release. Whether I knew or did not know, or how much or how little I knew, is totally unimportant when I consider what horrors I ought to have known about and what conclusions would have been the natural ones to draw from the little I did know. Those who ask me are fundamentally expecting me to offer justifications. But I have none. No apologies are possible.[25]

As far as I'm concerned, that passage needs no comment, but it has drawn a lot of the "He had to have known" fire. We ask how far we can believe him when he claims he did not know how bad it was at Dachau, did not know the destination of those trainloads of Jews being pulled out of his factories to the complaints of managers in desperate need of their skills and "relocated" to the east, that he did not know, did not know, did not know....

This passage is met with insistences that he did know, had to know, must have known. I would personally have found it unspeakably painful to bear the amount of responsibility he offered to carry, and did — let alone the weight his critics are so eager to add. Mercy had a lot to work on, and the responsibility he accepted was more than enough to darken his psychological world for the rest of his life.

Truth and Guilt

I have said, as I believe, that the issue of what Speer knew is irrelevant to the process of conversion. But are we compelled by evidence to conclude that he *did* know — in any of the forms proposed? In other words, does the evidence prevent us from taking him more or less at his word?

The first form proposed is that of the deliberate lie. I know that to many people, this is a foregone conclusion. But I am convinced that thoughtful assessment of the evidence tells against the deliberate lie. For one thing, if he were deliberately lying, the complexity of structure needed to sustain this kind of deception boggles my common sense. And he could hardly have become the kind of man I am assured he was by persons whose spiritual perception I trust.

What about the repression theory? We know that repression is possible and that an endangered psyche can shut down at some point of pressure that threatens survival. We don't do this consciously, and our access to the knowledge afterward is very limited. Yes, it's a possibility, and I leave the possibility open, but again, the evidence to me is not conclusive.

Of its very nature, truth in this case does not yield to circumstantial evidence, which is all we have. And too much of the answer lies in the area of the psychological and the spiritual, which is known only to God. Looking on from outside, we can but sort the probabilities, and we should do so with proper respect for the mystery at the center of this man's life.

The Third Option

The third choice is that, strangely enough, he really could be telling the truth. It might be that by working at it, and even perhaps by Hitler's own shielding intent, he did escape knowledge of the extermination policy. Personally I have witnessed examples of denial so blood-curdling that had I not been intimately connected with the situations in question, I could not have imagined self-deception so massive and impenetrable.

To express it awkwardly, if it's possible to repress what we do know, it should be equally possible to avoid knowing in the first place. The vision in our tunnel can be sharp enough; it's what's outside that does not exist.

He did, as he freely admits, know a great deal. The death camps did not emerge like mushrooms after a rainy night. They were the end product of a cumulative process of outrage upon Jews, gypsies, and other "inferior" and undesirable human beings. These preparatory phases were known to Speer. He saw the "Do not buy from Jews" on shop windows, rode into cities under anti-Semitic banners, wrestled with "emigration" problems, and listened to the verbal vomit of Hitler's speeches — or, perhaps worse, the casual remarks slipped into dinner conversation between the soup and the fish. He himself assisted in the violation of conquered peoples by accepting and encouraging Saukel's inhumane methods of conscription. Things were bad enough before and beside Mauthausen.

He saw, he heard, and he must have feared what he did not know. We see him refusing to question Hanke's broken story of Auschwitz. That door must not be opened, so he set his weight against it.

But even what he actually saw and heard need not have registered correctly in the brain to which it was available. It's possible not to see what's there and not to hear what's being said. How many of us regular church-goers are distinguished veterans of uncountable nonheard sermons? The reasons he gives (and some he does not) are logical. Attachment to his position with Hitler and the one-track way he ran his job could deflect any threat to the fulfillment of what had become a consuming emotional need. His known closeness to Hitler could prevent people from being honest with him.

Even throughout his imprisonment, he clung to his "excuses" for not having known. As reasons, they were real enough and assist our own understanding of him, but by the time he finished his memoirs, he was to see that though they explained how he could have achieved denial, they did not excuse him for

choosing to deny. He had to admit that excuses like these did
not excuse:

> ... that in Hitler's system, as in every totalitarian regime,
> when a man's position rises, his isolation increases and he
> is therefore more sheltered from harsh reality; that with
> the application of technology to the process of murder the
> number of murderers is reduced and therefore the possi-
> bility of ignorance grows; that the craze for secrecy built
> into the system creates degrees of awareness, so it is easy
> to escape observing inhuman cruelties.[26]

What was at fault was his basic orientation of not wanting to
know, the setting of his face against a knowledge that he could
and should have had.

People dealing with Hitler dealt with unreality. When they
wanted to persist in this exchange of the real for the unreal, they
learned not to call themselves immoral or insane. It was not
really easy to escape observing, but if one tried hard enough —
and surely he did — I have no reason to deny that it could
be done.

> It has repeatedly surprised me, in later years, that scarcely
> any anti-Semitic remarks of Hitler's have remained in my
> memory. Out of the scraps that remain, I can reconstruct
> what crossed my mind at the time: dismay over the devi-
> ation from the image I wanted to have of Hitler, anxiety
> over the increasing deterioration of his health, hope for
> some letup of the struggle against the churches, a certain
> puzzlement at his partiality for utopian-sounding remote
> goals, all sorts of odd feelings — but Hitler's hatred for
> the Jews seemed to me so much a matter of course that I
> gave it no serious thought.[27]

What about the grace of God? A man so open to the anguish of an awakened conscience, a man who spent twenty
solitary years in confrontation with the reality that stood behind what he called a hall of self-deceiving mirrors: would God
have denied him the opportunity to know, accept, and repent

the whole of his sin, to live through the last dreadful hour before the dawn?

We cannot say what God would do, for God has common sense as well as we. To leave a last defense, to let someone substitute a lesser burden for one too great for the emotional system to bear, and still to set in motion the work of mercy within a real desire for truth: all this God can do. But we do not have to assume that this was what happened. "Could have been" is not a synonym for "was."

If I seem to be making unnecessarily heavy water of something that makes no difference in the scale of guilt and restitution — for Speer considered himself as guilty as if he had himself directed the program of atrocity — I have a reason.

Our Own Choice of Self-Deceit

By whatever stratagems of ignorance, Speer got what he wanted, when what he did not want and warded off was what he needed most.

The Gospel of John speaks of "loving the dark," and we think "they" and not "we." At his cost and that of the world he mangled, Albert Speer instructs us in the tragic ease with which we, all of us, can kill the light that threatens to save us from what we have determined to have. And if he truly "did not know," how like to us this is. For most of us are less in danger of direct and knowing collusion with evil than of "not knowing" it is there. We can choose the dark; we can want it, and work hard at shutting out the light. And later we can honestly say we did not see. The contemplation of Albert Speer's self-blinded journey into horror can sharpen our perception of what we ought to know.

> *I have always thought it was a most valuable trait to recognize reality and not to pursue delusions. But when I now think over my life up to and including the years of imprisonment, there was no period in which I was free of delusory notions.*

The departure from reality, which was visibly spreading like a contagion, was no peculiarity of the National Socialist regime. But in normal circumstances people who turn their backs on reality are soon set straight by the mockery and criticism of those around them, which makes them aware they have lost credibility. In the Third Reich there were no such correctives, especially for those who belonged to the upper stratum. On the contrary, every self-deception was multiplied as in a hall of distorting mirrors, becoming a repeatedly confirmed picture of a fantastical dream world which no longer bore any relationship to the grim outside world. In those mirrors I could see nothing but my own face reproduced many times over. No external factors disturbed the uniformity of hundreds of unchanging faces, all mine.

There were differences of degree in the flight from reality. Thus Goebbels was surely many times closer to recognizing actualities than, say, Goering or Ley. But these differences shrink to nothing when we consider how remote all of us, the illusionists as well as the so-called realists, were from what was really going on.[28]

He could have known. That in itself is terrible. That is what he admitted and lived with for thirty-six years.

Chapter 6

Enlightenment

If Hitler had won the war, would Speer have been lost in the marble world of the great new German Reich? Probably. He'd have pocketed the shreds of his conscience, built his Great Hall, and died without a glance at his wasted heart. It's doubtful that he would even have suspected the layer of human bones under the foundations of his buildings.

As it happened, success did not starve out his capacity for self-knowledge. It was fed, but gradually, with defeat and disillusion. The German military situation deteriorated under a policy which he could recognize as increasingly more irresponsible and insane. It didn't take unusual intelligence to see that most of the trouble lay with Hitler's insistence on overriding professional military judgment. Speer was an intimate witness to the personal disintegration of the Fuehrer whom he had worshiped as a mythic savior, the semi-divine rescuer of his country's destiny. I have said there was something very young in this technocrat.

The Crack Widens

Infighting among Hitler's followers almost cost Speer his life during an illness of which Himmler took advantage to attempt his murder. Weeks of physical incapacity and absence from the power center of the Reich returned him to some degree of perspective. Later, in Spandau, he was to remember that the first weakening of his devotion to Hitler was rooted in aesthetics:

Seeing [Hitler] again after an interval of ten weeks, I was for the first time in all the years I had known him struck

*by his overly broad nose and sallow color. I realized that
his whole face was repulsive — the first sign that I was
beginning to attain some perspective and see him with un-
biased eyes. For almost a quarter of a year I had not been
exposed to his personal influence but instead to his insults
and reprimands. After years of frenzy and fever I had for
the first time begun to think about the course I was pursu-
ing at his side.... All I wanted was to go to Meran with
my wife and children as soon as possible; I wanted to
spend many weeks there, to recover my strength. But I did
not really know what I wanted my strength for, because I
no longer had a goal.*[29]

That was not the end, of course. Not to have a goal wasn't
enough. But a more realistic appraisal of Hitler's exterior features could lead to a more realistic view of his inner features
as well. And a true acquaintance with that inner world was to
bring to Albert Speer the terrible gift of self-revelation: here was
the monster to whom he had given his service and his life.

The enlightenment continued on a graduated course. The
attempted coup of July 1944 brought Speer under suspicion,
though he had neither known of it nor taken part. He recalls
honestly his relief at being cleared and once again received
into Hitler's inner circle — again like a school kid desperate
to belong to the gang, or an executive with the schoolboy's
emotional system, needing his place in the administration.

Yet the crack was widening, and light was creeping through.

Into his readiness broke Hitler's decision to destroy Germany,
to bring the nation down with himself into what he correctly
called the abyss. Speer's informants here were Walter Rohland,
the industrialist, and Willy Liebel, a department head in the
Armaments Ministry.

*This was the first time that the specter of "scorched earth"
loomed before me. For Rohland went on to speak of the
fear that a desperate top leadership might order wholesale
destruction. Then and there, on that day, I felt something
stirring within me that was quite apart from Hitler: a sense*

of responsibility toward the country and the people to save as much as possible of our industrial potential, so that the nation could survive the period after a lost war. But for the present it was still a vague and shadowy sense.[30]

Liebel drew the picture of what the Fuehrer's latest edict meant. No German was to inhabit territory occupied by the enemy. Those wretches who did remain would find themselves in a desert devoid of all the amenities of civilization. Not only the industrial plants, and not only the gas, water, electrical works and telephone exchanges were to be completely smashed. Everything, simply everything essential to the maintenance of life would be destroyed: the ration card records, the files of marriage and resident registeries, the records of bank accounts. In addition, food supplies were to be destroyed, farms burned down and cattle killed. Not even those works of art that the bombs had spared were to be preserved. Monuments, palaces, castles and churches, theaters and opera houses were also to be leveled. A few days earlier, at Hitler's command, an editorial had appeared, putting this surge of vandalism into rhetoric: "Not a German stalk of wheat is to feed the enemy, not a German mouth to give him information, not a German hand to offer him help. He is to find every footbridge destroyed, every road blocked — nothing but death, annihilation, and hatred will meet him."[31]

Hitler went further, ordering German withdrawal to the center of the country, with no provision for survival, no shelter or food or hygienic resources. The fact that this order could actually have been taken seriously gives some indication of the mental state created in Germany by the psychological mechanism of the Third Reich.

Speer was not buying this. It is interesting that the practical technician in him, that strong component of his personality which had played so decided a part in his moral imprisonment, here broke loose and asserted itself on the side of truth. The man of common sense realized that his country should not be sacrificed to the disappointed megalomania of its demoralized leader. He wanted his country to survive, and he was practical enough to ensure this. Hitler had taken him a fair way to hell, but when Speer finally stopped and turned, he could still find the road back to reason, humanity, and grace.

The Technician Transformed

Seeing, however, was not enough. The road back had to be taken.

> *After a few restless hours I walked across the fields and climbed a hill. The village lay peacefully below me in the sunlight under a thin veil of mist. I could see far out over the hills of Sauerland, the land lying between the Sieg and the Ruhr rivers. How was it possible, I thought, that one man wanted to transform this land into a desert. I lay down in the fern. Everything seemed unreal. But the soil gave off a spicy fragrance; the first green sprouts of plants were springing from the ground. As I walked back, the sun was setting. I had taken my resolve. The execution of that order must be prevented.[32]*

I love this text, for the seasonal and rural setting evoke a sense of Easter, and we are dealing here with the resurrection of a human heart. He was to claim later that this stage of opposition to Hitler was the action of a technician and not of a Christian. This is true enough, but in another sense, had not God appropriated all of this man's personality? Were his technical skill and mentality any less the property of the creator than the deeper qualities he was later to develop? God used what was to hand. He used all of Speer there was. At this moment, the technical Speer came in handy, and the technical Speer was no less a member of Christ than the man who was to study theology in a prison cell.

He did one thing at a time, and — as Newman found — in following his conscience through one act after another, light grew in proportion to his fidelity to it. We have to start somewhere, and Speer began where he could: by using as a free man the skills which had so long imprisoned him.

It's important to see that his first response to the light of reality was active. He *did* something, and he did it in the ruins of personal ambition, and of the emotional attachment to Hitler which had provided the primary motivation of his life. He acted even in what he now recognized as the ruins of his own moral constitution.

His motivation was salvific and other-centered, to the extent that it could be so at that time of stumbling back into rectitude and humaneness. He wanted to save his country, to provide a material foundation for the rebuilding of Germany, and in this effort to provide some kind of reparation for the devastation to which he had himself subjected her.

I said "to the extent." Of course there was plenty of self-seeking in this course of action. Why not? He wanted to show (grandstanding again) that he had salvaged at least some of the moral stature he had been dumping with such consistent energy. And it was his own country which was the object of his saving efforts, after he had played so heavy a part in wrecking the rest of the world. But acknowledging this self-centered component of his motivation did not prevent him from acting.

When the need and opportunity for action ran out, when he seemed to have no further gift for the country he had so badly betrayed, he could at least reject both suicide and flight, and accept responsibility for his role in the leadership of the Third Reich. This acceptance of responsibility was to become his sacred vocation, a slowly moving river into which the twisting currents of his life poured themselves out.

He had not expected to be tried with the first rank of Nazi war criminals. But the Allies knew how important his work had been; and so he came to Nuremberg to face the War Crimes Trial and its bitter months of evidence:

> *To this day photographs, documents, and orders keep coming back to me. They were so monstrous that they*

*seemed unbelievable, and yet none of the defendants
doubted their genuineness.*[33]

Someone with whom I was talking about Speer asked, "How
could he, how *could* he have gone on living?"

He did not appeal his sentence, the "Albert Speer, to twenty
years..." but accepted it as "fair enough." Years later, he was
to request amnesty, encouraging his friends and family to obtain a shortening of his sentence. But even then, he could not
ask with a single mind, so convinced was he of the necessity to
suffer out his punishment. The amnesty was denied, of course.
The Soviets would not permit it.

And so to the last minute of the last day of its last year, he
lived out his sentence at Spandau, those "years without event"
in which God supervised the slow and subtle transformation
of a master technician into a humble and transparent human
being, a man of compassion and spiritual depth.

Photos of Speer's Nazi career convey his vigor, his youth,
strength, and good looks. But there is something hard in his
face, something unformed and undeveloped. The photos of his
release from prison are at first shocking: he looks far older than
his sixty years. But under the white hair and the dark peaked
brows, his translucent eyes and remarkable smile witness to a
transformed heart. A close friend of his last years has said to
me, "Yes, he had beautiful eyes" — eyes that had learned to see.

She also says of him that he was holy. And we will get to this.

Chapter 7

And We Too

Self-knowledge for Speer meant far more than, "I did this. I am morally responsible for the brutality of a regime whose power I fostered and shared." Self-knowledge in our case is far more than coming clear on what bad things we have done and are responsible for and still might do. It's more than recognizing the dangers that still threaten us from within ourselves, and even more than getting an effective view of our psychological make-up.

Self-knowledge at this point is the beginning of a journey into something which remains self-knowledge while deepening into several kinds of relationship, for we cannot really know ourselves except in relation to Christ and to all that we presently think of as other than ourselves.

A journey. You would expect the journey to start — well, somewhere, and proceed to some other place, perhaps slowly, but at least purposefully and with deliberate and straight-forward progress. And when you got where you were going, you would be there, and stay there, and your only problem from then on would be responding to the light, light which would hang around for the rest of your life. It doesn't happen that way. The light of self-knowledge is subject to eclipse. The ambitions that veiled it from the beginning sneak back or race back and we sit there in the dark — or are very active in the dark — until the lights go on again. At least we trust that they will.

How to Avoid It

Many things in life are difficult. They take effort, skill, determination, and perseverance. Avoiding self-knowledge is not one. All it takes is to want something else: to want it *more* than we want to know ourselves, yes, but even just wanting will do. We want something so much, and often so desperately, that we cannot face not having it. And even though we see self-knowledge as a good, the power of our need for something else convinces us that we do see, we do know quite enough about ourselves to pray well, choose well, act well.

Our judgment and our standards of value have been taken over by the ache for this whatever-it-is that we have decided will stop a need from hurting. It has become the meaning of our life, the "who" of us. This satisfaction is the ointment which can, we are sure, soothe a kind of generalized psychic rash, which, we don't realize, is growing more invasive the longer we keep it soothed.

Therefore we cannot see.

It's not the desire that's wrong, as if not-wanting were the road to self-knowledge. It's the disproportion between the object of our wanting and the state of our mind and feelings. The classical word is "attachment," but that has ominous overtones, as if we were meant to deposit our emotional life in a lead box and lock it up for life.

Ambition

Part of our trouble then lies in wanting something so radically that it disrupts the balance of our personality. Part of our problem lies in the disruption of another kind of balance: we want a good which in its present setting is not a good for *us* — to covet the neighbor's wife, his ox or his ass, to covet the neighbor's status.

Both these factors come into play when ambition is the desire in question. Nothing is wrong with ambition. It's a natural drive to cooperate with God's purpose in giving us our particular set of abilities.

A good shot of ambition can forestall any number of tragedies. I've read of a high school athletic coach whose technique reaches not only into the physical, but also into the moral and emotional fiber of his players. They're learning both athletic and moral skills: how to set goals, meet challenges, handle success as well as failure. This is ambition at its best, a road to human excellence.

But we're in trouble with ambition at less than its best: not only desire for the good that is not good for us, but desire erected into the scaffolding of our personality, a habit of appraising ourselves by way of comparison. I can carry around the conviction that I am important because of how I rate in comparison with someone else. Someone else's position becomes the measure of my worth, and so I build my importance on the inferiority of others.

Or I spend my life trying to fight my way out of a sense of inferiority by way of being "as good as" someone else or belonging, as Speer was emotionally compelled to belong, to an elite group of insiders.

What Do I Really Want?

I may be young enough to consider the possible heights. What about the corporate ladder — or some other form of metaphorical gold braid? On the other hand, one of the lessons of Spandau, as one of the lessons of monastic life, is that if big opportunities are wanting, little ones will do. Very little.

It's amazing the character of the things from which we draw our daily psychic nourishment. And the less secure we feel about our personal selves, the more desperately we clutch at the petty and inconsequential, and the harder we fight off any interference with whatever small importances we have used to build a self with. Those of us in monastic life know how often this is the trouble with obedience. It's not just that doing what you're told can seem inconvenient or humiliating, but that it's a terrible threat to these interwoven networks of self-establishment.

What we really want, of course, is to be.

And achievement gives us a hearty sense of being. It should; it's meant to. Neither as individuals nor as community would we find ourselves in a good place without achievement. Yet an unbalanced desire for achievement becomes a detour around self-knowledge and a substitute for growth, endangering the very being we are trying to secure.

Status

In a marvelous prayer, John Wesley offers to serve as a drawer of water or a hewer of wood so that he may dwell in the house of the Lord. Why does it hurt to be nobody? Why would Wesley have used this wonderful image but for the deep human reluctance to remain in a position so low that there is no one left to be one's inferior? Something in us fights the fact that our importance does not rest on someone else's inferiority, especially since we would like to think of it as our superiority.

Achievement of itself is not status, nor status the inevitable result of achievement. We have to be fairly adept at separating these two objects of desire, so often interwoven that the one can be sought for the sake of the other.

And we have to be even more adept at recognizing the more refined types of status, the longing which can bypass material, intellectual, or artistic glory in order to experience itself as spiritually secure: "as good as," or "better than" the mature, experienced, and respected "spiritual" people. We can want the by-products of a spiritual outlook: feeling oneself emotionally mature, with eyes sharp enough and wits experienced enough to spot the self-deceits and analyze the revealing behavior of others, to make comfortable allowances for those with less self-knowledge, to identify with a certain level of balance and prayerfulness.

Why does it hurt to realize, when we've reached an age we've unconsciously ticketed as a kind of cut-off point, that we're going to be stuck with most of what's wrong with us until we die, that the daily job of handling our own inner share of human complication will go on with humiliating regularity as long as our hearts beat and our brain waves operate? Why do we mind so much when our contemporaries or juniors seem to have reached an interior level we can only look at from below, or are trusted with pastoral charges we know we would blow if we had them? At one point we set out to be humble, to rejoice at being lowly and unhonored, and now look. Why? We want to *be,* and we have absorbed somewhere the certainty that in order to be we must secure the right position relative to other people. Above them if we can, but belonging to the in-group if we can't.

When We Stop Running Out

The point, however, is not how many ways are available for escaping self-knowledge, but what happens in the crunch, when we agree to stop and look, and not only to see but also to give over what we see to a God who has known all along what we are just beginning to acknowledge.

The crunch might be, outwardly, very serious, or quite a modest event, or even, as we will be seeing shortly, a non-event. Perhaps it's someone else's promotion or someone else's sturdy display of virtue, or a birthday with which I have some quarrel. It could be success that opens on the dreary landscape of, "Is this all?" Or maybe the boss is changed, and the boss is not me. Perhaps the work load has been redistributed or the team reshuffled. A marriage may have reached the stage of desperation, or its adolescent children may be close to suicide.

My reaction is asking me to stop and pay attention, to see, to acknowledge, and to choose. I can refuse to see; I've got along this far, muddling and denying and falling into familiar patterns of taking care — somehow — of how I feel or refuse to feel. I can continue to manipulate my situation to make myself feel less awful, or play for sympathy, or hate myself, or grab at any of the various other opportunities I am accustomed to taking advantage of.

Actually, I can bring up a well-constructed spiritual justification for some kinds of refusal to see, or for the wrong way of handling what I do see. Or I can stop, really stop, and say with Albert Speer: Yes, this is my self; this is what I have done and am. I accept responsibility for myself.

The door then opens onto another choice.

What Do I Do with What I Am?

I can choose to offer others the gift of trying to live by noncomparison. "I do not need your inferiority in order to prove my worth." Or, "I will not hang on to the coat-tails of your importance, as a substitute for my own. I give you my respect in the refusal to use you for the advancement of my need to be."

To myself, I offer the truth. And truth, for us as for Speer, has a double nature. It guides and it embraces.

It guides. For surely we are going somewhere. We are moving from darkness into light, though at first the light seems to be nothing but darkness, the darkness of our own hearts. We can squirm and agonize, we can struggle with despair. One of the great advantages of knowing Albert Speer is the relief of knowing ourselves accompanied through this encounter with dark light: "He's been here before me, and thank God I'll never have to go through what he did." We can know to the point of tasting it, the debased and deprived self who can identify with Nazi Germany and a great deal more. We can turn the page rather too fast on a reference to Katyn Forest. But though we agree to the awful part, the dark thickets and the stench, we have to believe that this is not the end, not the revelation of our real being. We must walk through the fragility and the guilt, but to the acknowledgment of our true dignity. For in offering our wounds to the ministering, accepting touch of God, we know them as the festering wounds of Christ, destined to become the holy and glorious wounds of Easter Day.

As one who has been made a partner in the Paschal Mystery and as one who has been configured to the death of Christ, [all men of good will in whose hearts grace is active invisibly] will go forward, strengthened by hope, to the resurrection.[34]

Truth also embraces. Self-knowledge is communion with God, a place we are invited into. The door is opened and we may walk in. Or we may walk by, or walk in and out. We may prefer to forget there is such a door. But if we allow ourselves to be let in, escorted in, usually by uncomfortable companions and embarrassing circumstances, we find more than our unappealing manifestations of self-interest.

We find our own beauty and we find God's, because the light of truth is the self-revelation of Christ. The best way of knowing our own beauty is by knowing God, whose image we are, and knowing him as mercy. This is the only way there: through knowledge of our own fragility and guilt to the acknowledgment of our own true majesty. If we try to short-circuit the awful part, the banality of our unresponsiveness, if we try to shove it aside and go directly to the pure center of our identity in Christ, we don't make it. We've got this shadow in back of us, or moving in from the side and threatening to smother the glory at any minute. We can't go to the beauty of ourselves without heading directly into that cloud.

By this I do not mean cultivating depression and self-abuse. "Whatever you have done to the least of my brethren...." Our self-abuse is abuse of Christ; it is ingratitude and falsity. There is a self-denigration which is distinctly unhealthy, and one of those switches by which emotional disability takes over a constructive value and trains it to serve its own distorted ends. Humility is not self-hatred. Self-knowledge is not self-castigation.

Christ is the light by which a series of ordinary occurrences has made clear the litter on the road we have been following. But the light of Christ is his own being, his desire to know and be known by us in deep and simple intimacy. And here we are, stuck in this light, stuck in the uncomfortable business of learning our own glory. What to do?

Don't go away.

For if the light has to come through the broken beams and shattered corridors of our misguided ambitions, the light is Christ, and it's okay to see.

I wanted to walk once more through the neighboring Chancellery, which I had built. Since the lights were no longer functioning, I contented myself with a few farewell minutes in the Court of Honor, whose outlines could scarcely be seen against the night sky. I sensed rather than saw the architecture. There was an almost ghostly quiet about everything, like a night in the mountains. The noise of a great city, which in earlier years had penetrated to here even during the night, had totally ceased. At rather long intervals I heard the detonations of Russian shells. Such was my last visit to the Chancellery. Years ago I had built it — full of plans, prospects, and dreams for the future. Now I was leaving the ruins of my building, and of the most significant years of my life.[35]

On July 16, 1945, seventy-eight months after the dedication, Winston Churchill was shown through the Chancellery. "In front of the Chancellery," [he wrote], "there was a considerable crowd. When I got out of the car and walked among them, except for one old man who shook his head disapprovingly, they all began to cheer. My hate had died with their surrender, and I was much moved by their demonstrations." Then the party walked for a good while through the shattered corridors and halls of the Chancellery. Soon afterward the remains of the building were removed. The stone and marble supplied the materials for the Russian war monument in Berlin-Treptow.[36]

Part II

The Garden

Chapter 8

The Garden

Feb. 5, 1949. The days pass swiftly and leave little memorable behind. Today ten wild geese flew across my small segment of sky. First signs of spring. The buds are fat on our lilac bush.[37]

What does God do with our response to self-knowledge, with our sorrow and acknowledgment of responsibility? God forgives.

And forgiveness is not the doorsill of a love that lies somewhere beyond itself. Mercy is the quality of an embrace tempered to the need of a wounded heart. Mercy is love's second name.[38]

Why do we so often find this an unsatisfactory way of being loved? It's not that we are unappreciative of being forgiven. We need it, and we know that. Who would want to run around unforgiven? It's the continual quality of our need for it that we face unwillingly, that we find hard to integrate into our understanding of love. Why can't this love God offers so abundantly be neater, better organized, more logical? We know more or less where we stand, but the footing is too slippery for comfort. Why, in a word, do we need to be forgiven so often?

And isn't it incomplete? Forgiven — well, yes, but you can get so tired of a landscape that never seems to change. We'd prefer it to be over all at once, and then you could get on with life, and climb to new and purer pastures instead of breathing the air of forgiveness moment by moment, day after day, of never feeling, "Hey, this was a nice, well-packaged act of virtue."

For some reason — what reason? — the Jesus Prayer, whether we say it or not, is the great fact of our life. Have mercy. "Lord

Jesus Christ, have mercy on me. Now. Now. Ever. In your mercy
I place my today, my yesterday, and my tomorrow. Let them not
squirm there. In loving you, I love forgiveness."

> Do you not know that all of us who have been baptized
> into Christ Jesus were baptized into his death? Therefore
> we have been buried with him by baptism into death, so
> that, just as Christ was raised from the dead by the glory
> of the Father, so we too might walk in newness of life.
> For if we have been united with him in a death like his,
> we will certainly be united with him in a resurrection like
> his. We know that our old self was crucified with him so
> that the body of sin might be destroyed, and we might no
> longer be enslaved to sin. For whoever has died is freed
> from sin. But if we have died with Christ, we believe that
> we will also live with him. The death he died, he died to
> sin, once for all; but the life he lives, he lives to God. So
> you also must consider yourselves dead to sin and alive to
> God in Christ Jesus. (Rom. 6:3–11 NRSV)

That We Too Might Live a New Life

Our baptism, in a sense, is always going on. We are always being enfolded in that exquisite moment of grace, always being
born, always being washed and new and fresh. It's not as if we
got all this good stuff and stood there with our candle in a white
robe and felt like spring, like weddings and sunrises and first
loves. And then we start walking and falling down and climb-
ing and stumbling, and the candle gets lost and our knees bleed
and we're all over sweat, and, "Oh, Lord, where's my baptism,
somewhere a million years ago?"

It's not like that at all. Say we're stepping into a church, and
we realize that this building is more than itself. It's a cool quiet
lake, washing off the blood and healing the hurt, and giving
us new birth this moment. Say we stop a moment at work, to
look at the tractor or computer or washer under our hands,
and know that this is lit from inside by that baptismal candle.

And all the self-centered choices and slips of disposition that are brought to its flame are fuel for the light it gives. "I'm sorry," is not a burden but a bonfire.

There's no neat theological way of saying it, except that the sacraments reach into eternity, into timelessness, into the eternal moment of our redemption, and draw us into it. Baptism is now, Reconciliation, the Eucharist. They aren't back there when we were nice. They aren't yesterday or this morning. They are this moment, because the paschal mystery which they express and mediate is eternal.

Baptism is the churchly ratification, the celebration of faith's encounter with Jesus' eternal redemptive gift. All the sacramental life of the church is a presence to that moment, a reaching out for it, a grasping of it. This *now,* if we but want and realize it, is the bestowal of grace to reach out and claim our sacramental inheritance. Forgiveness is sacramental even at its most inward, quiet, hidden, and personal. It is always churchly and communal. But this is abstract. How can we be more concrete?

The Garden as Symbol

I said at the beginning that the symbol of imprisonment evolved into several other symbols in the life of Albert Speer. We have seen one: the builder. Now in an exploration of forgiveness, we find another: the garden.

Gardens are crafted, the product of God's bounty and human hands, brains, backs, and sweat. They answer several human needs, one of which is the need for a richly symbolic life. The garden, as a matter of fact, offers itself as an image of God. For in a garden, every sense is pleased, and some sort of satisfaction is extended to every need. There is food, provided you are growing raspberries as well as marigolds. It provides shelter, beauty, peace, creative labor, and a place in which to develop the joys of companionship. The garden sustains, nourishes, and challenges. It must also be hauled out of the wild, at the cost of much sacrifice and some blood. It is this wholeness that says to us that a garden is a reflection of God. But that does not exhaust its symbolic function.

Innocence Lost and Found

For us who are inheritors of Genesis, a garden typifies innocence and the loss of it; for the Lord God planted a garden, and set in it, to plant and tend its abundance, a man and a woman whose joy was as clear as the blue running brooks at their feet. Then when that joy had dissolved into guilt, a garden wrapped its shadowing arms around their shame.

But a garden drank up the first blood of their Savior's Passion, and in Lanier's familiar and beautiful words:

> Into the woods my Master went,
> clean forspent, forspent.
> Into the woods my Master came,
> forspent with love and shame.
> But the olives they were not blind to him,
> the little grey leaves were kind to him,
> The thorn-tree had a mind to him,
> when into the woods he came.
>
> Out of the woods my Master went,
> and he was well content.
> Out of the woods my Master came,
> content with death and shame.
> When death and shame would woo him last,
> from under the trees they drew him last:
> 'twas on a tree they slew him — last,
> when out of the woods he came.

> —Sydney Lanier, "The Tree and the Master"

It received, according to John, his dead body — and his resurrection. For Mary thought he was the gardener (John 20:15).

> My beloved has gone down to his garden,
> to the beds of spices,

> to pasture his flock in the gardens,
>   and to gather lilies.
> I am my beloved's and my beloved
>   is mine;
> he pastures his flock among the lilies.
>   (Song of Solomon 6:2b–3 NRSV)

Speer's Garden

Albert Speer was an artist, accustomed, in the masculine mode, to the making of beauty. We traditionally attribute to male artists a rather easy access to the anima, the feminine principle existing in both men and women. And yet Speer's psychic make-up would seem to have been overbalanced toward the masculine. His life had been spent with men, and the Nazi ethos in which he was caught up was admittedly, even disastrously, male. He was an administrative genius, a man of technology, and his particular field of creative endeavor involved the massive, the hard, and the resistant. His milieu was stone and metal and the articulation of space.

Now he built a garden. If we think of gardens as feminine, we are only half right, but perhaps this effort was a work of personal integration as well as a work of beauty. Perhaps Speer's preoccupation with the earth and growing plants was a redemption of the disproportionately aggressive and brutal character of the culture he had accepted so blindly. At any rate, his experience of earth, seasons, and growth is an exact image of every conversion.

"Built" and "work," however, are appropriate words for this architect's creation in plants. It was a creation of hard labor.

I can now do whatever I please in my part of the garden. In the spring I dug out the ground to a depth of about half a meter, and created a sunken rock garden; using thousands of bricks, I made a series of retaining walls twenty to forty centimeters in height. I brought all the bricks from an unused part of the prison area by wheelbarrow, for the sake of exercise. "What are you going to do with all those bricks?" Neurath asked. "This is the first time I've ever seen anyone carting bricks into a garden."[39]

In intense heat, every other day I carry fifty full watering cans, each holding ten liters of water, to the plants I set in the spring. This amounts to moving a load of five hundred liters, or half a metric ton. I can be content: of the sixty plants I set out in the spring, only two have died.[40]

Sometimes I think of all I could have done in these years. Now I produce paths in the prison garden, meditations on crime and punishment, or silly nonsense.[41]

He didn't really know what he was doing; he didn't know that this activity was saying more about his life than he himself understood. What was Paradise to him who could not believe himself innocent? He did it to condition his mind and body, and as a form of creative expression. What do you do when you're an architect and you're in prison? What do you do with the mind and body formed by your profession and your genetic heritage and your cultural conditioning? If you get the chance, you make something beautiful. You build a garden, and do it the hard way.

About two years ago, in response to [Colonel] Cuthill's invitation, I systematically set about landscaping our garden, making a park of it. I graded uneven ground into interesting terraces, sowed lawns, planted forsythia, lavender, hydrangea bushes, and roses. In addition I set out twenty-five lilacs of my own raising. Along the paths I have laid out beds of iris two and a half meters wide and fifty meters long. Today seedling pines, birches, and lindens were delivered. With such a wealth of plant materials I can begin to lay out a landscape garden.

No one interferes. During the past few weeks I have made many sketches, trying to visualize my park in its completed form. But I know that no landscape gardener has ever seen in nature what was present to his mind's eye. Trees, bushes, flowers and grass take too long to grow together into a landscape. But I want to see at least the beginnings of the thing I am working for here day after day with such obstinate passion. And so I must hope to remain here long enough to witness nature's realization of my plans; but at the same time I fear that very thing. Spandau has become a meaning in itself. Long ago I had to organize my survival here. That is no longer necessary. The garden has taken full possession of me.[42]

And if God guides the enterprise, it says more than you meant it to.

Acceptance of Forgiveness

We have seen the stance Speer took toward his guilt: honesty, acceptance of responsibility and of punishment, reparation, vicarious expiation for others. The one missing piece is something he was poorly instructed in: the acceptance of forgiveness.

I have heard someone say of him, "How could he ever forgive himself?" I think he never did; or rather, he simply didn't think that way. Even a realization of the full measure of God's forgiveness seems to have been impossible for him. Someone else asked me, "Did he ever believe himself forgiven?" Again, I wonder whether the question, posed in that way, would have made sense to him. The extent of the mercy with which God cleansed and adorned his heart lay far beyond the reach of his rational faculties, so that he seems not to have been able to acknowledge it in a pure form. But to mercy in a mediated form, he did reach humbled hands and bring them back brim full. It would have been so easy to retreat into the complicated mechanisms of guilt and a vastly damaged self-esteem; but through the everyday sacrament of human kindness, offered and received, he was accepting an infinite if unrecognized mercy.

During the next twenty years of my life, I was guarded, in Spandau Prison, by nationals of the four powers against whom I had organized Hitler's war. Along with my six fellow-prisoners, they were the only people I had close contact with. Through them I learned directly what the effects of my work had been. Many of them mourned loved ones who had died in the war — in particular, every one of the Soviet guards had lost some close relative, brothers or a father. Yet not one of them bore a grudge toward me for my personal share in the tragedy; never did I hear words of recrimination. At the lowest ebb of my existence, in contact with these ordinary people, I encountered uncorrupted feelings of sympathy, helpfulness, human understanding, feelings that bypassed the prison rules. On the day before my appointment as Minister of Armaments and War Production I had encountered peasants in the Ukraine who had saved me from frostbite. At the time I had been merely touched, without understanding. Now, after all was over, I once again was treated to examples of human kindness that transcended all enmity. And now, at last, I wanted to understand.[43]

It was the reality of this forgiveness that he daily expressed in another kind of sacrament, the modest symbol of a garden. As he tended his linden trees, hauled bricks for terracing, planted beds of iris beside carefully planned walks, and made an old bathtub into a pool, he was acting out the drama of redemption. His garden was the visible expression of his redeemed self. God had restored Paradise in his heart.

Gardens as Forgiveness: The Feminine Aspect

Today an American soldier called down in English from the tower, "Mr. Speer, I like your garden. It's wonderful."[44]

I remember once using the familiar, even hackneyed image of the sea — another feminine symbol — to explain the relationship between love and forgiveness. The sea would be God's love; forgiveness was what happens when we turn and walk into it, or stop shivering on the pebbled shore or running around in the skirts of an incoming tide. The sea is always there, always itself: forgiveness is not a decision on God's part to be nice to somebody awful who has come to the point of reformation. Forgiveness is what happens when we walk right in and give ourselves to the waves and the gulls and the deep green mystery of this floorless ocean. It is love seen from the point of view of someone who has been afraid or unwilling to approach its wild, salt bounty.

But one May morning, as I was thinking about Speer's experience of forgiveness, I looked out the Chapter Room window into a monastic springtime. We have few cultivated flowering trees — lots of forsythia, a couple of magnolias. But spring in New England dispenses with human skills and makes the entire natural world into a garden. Maples, oaks, cottonwood, poplar are all blossoming in their way, then tiny leaves succeed sprays and tassels, becoming a kind of flower in themselves. The world is bronze, gold, chartreuse. In Robert Frost's little poem, "Nature's first green is gold, her hardest hue to hold...." This world of flowering leaf seemed to be offering itself as another image of forgiveness.

Mercy is like a garden in which we are always walking; it is our home, our native place. It is not a place we *go into,* but a place we are in and must take notice of. God is simple. God is not chopped up into attributes that have only a speaking knowledge of each other. Mercy *is* love. The difference is on our side, as the sea metaphor also tells us. But a garden encloses, holds us always, and to receive forgiveness, instead of turning and moving into it, we need but lift our eyes and acknowledge where we are. Once we do that, once we accept ourselves as embraced and loved and part of the splendor of the world in which we walk, there is no other course but to change the way of handling life which has blinded us to our true place in it.

Chapter 9

Growth

Restoration is generally a long work. Absolution is the business of a moment, but the reconstruction and healing of a damaged personality, the calling back of the divine likeness into a distorted human heart, proceeds neither quickly nor smoothly.

Gardens take time, effort, cultivation. They are a symbol of this drawing forth of material and spiritual creation from our personal chaos, a symbol of this moral and human restoration.

What happens then, in the hands of time? For one thing our values change:

> *I might even pursue the question further by asking whether Hitler — what a curious idea — is not the reason for my now, in prison, finding still another new identity. Without the experiences and insights I acquired as a result of those years with him, would I ever have learned that all historical grandeur means less than a modest gesture of humaneness; that all the national honor of which we dreamed is insignificant compared to simple readiness to help others? How strangely I find my viewpoints shifting.*[45]

Secondly, as we have already seen in considering Speer as an icon of redemption, restoration affects not only the self, but the world. Konrad Adenauer, who had opposed Hitler, and others whose collaboration had been less conspicuous and radical than Speer's, drew material, political, and economic order out of the postwar chaos. They rebuilt the Germany you can see. But at the same time, Speer, in his own personal reconstruction of soul, was secretly, doggedly, daily, and undramatically helping to draw the moral and spiritual order of Germany out of its ruins. In his own redeemed and redeeming self he was delivering the guilt of the world into the re-creative embrace of God.

That is the way conversion works. We cannot give over our own hearts to the pruning, planting, and cultivating action of God without taking with us the rest of the world. In the deepest part of ourselves, we share its soil, its rain and sun; and the only way we can isolate ourselves from the rest of the world is by refusing to surrender our own hearts to this work. For the process of seed, growth, and harvest go on within the paschal offering of Christ. He is our ground and our fruition.

God, who loved Albert Speer, let him fall that he might rise and, in his rising, help to bring his world back from its crushed moral cities and its desecrated lives. God, in whose hands coincidence so lightly rests, did not prevent the fatal contacts which led to this man's complicity in moral ruin — so that we might see there is nothing we can do that God is not eager to forgive, that his being is forgiveness as his being is love.

The Breadth of Re-creation

Thirty to sixty-five million people were killed in World War II. The gap in these statistics indicates the derangement of the world they tried to measure. How many more lives were damaged, mentally and physically, how many generations were warped and crippled emotionally? How great is the heritage with which we are now trying to deal?

This is real guilt, not just the icky feeling you get about yourself. And this is real forgiveness. We know that no one who does not seek it, who is not sorry, can enter this house of healing. But how many have come seeking because of Speer although they do not know it, and because of people like you and me trying to live out this asking? Another's grace depends on how completely I am willing to give myself to the work of my own inner re-creation.

I have said that we must forgive the repentant sinner. Just now I said that no one who does not seek it, who is not sorry, can enter this house of healing. But that leaves unsaid something that should have become obvious. Where does the repentance come from? It comes from the forgiveness that is there beforehand, that evokes and makes possible the repentance. Forgiveness waits for us to notice it is there. It asks our permission to create the repentance that will welcome the forgiveness and make conversion possible. God's forgiveness is like this, and God's forgiveness is the exemplar of our own.

Speer's own conversion obviously came from God. But since we are all so bound together, through what human agent did it come? I have wondered. Perhaps it was the gift of some great-hearted Jew. Or of some bewildered and anguished child of the gas chambers walking unexpectedly into the arms of God.

A Garden Is Beautiful

What is so beautiful about a man in prison? So he's forgiven? So what? So a lot of things, like the grandeur of personal accountability. Ask an alcoholic how good it feels to say, "Yes, I'm responsible." We are responsible because we are human, because our destiny is glorious. Accepting guilt is a celebration of the privilege of being free.

Beautiful too is the purity of not defending ourselves from truth, of facing our own moral weakness and so not defending ourselves from mercy and fulfillment. There is further beauty in the freedom of being able to let go of guilt, of permitting forgiveness to enter and remake us, letting ourselves grow into new creations. And this is not a facile sort of beauty, as we shall see.

The Problems

In turning over my compost heap I found a curled-up hedgehog who had settled down to hibernate there. I carefully put him into the wheelbarrow and transferred him to another compost heap at the other end of the garden. Now I will pile leaves on top of him.[46]

How peaceful, how gentle. Is all well in this garden world, or are there problems in Eden? Problems with forgiveness? Well, yes. And we've already touched them lightly. Forgiveness can act as a handy social tool, or the answer to a desperate need; we wouldn't want to live without it. But often, living with it is more difficult than we want it to be — and I am talking about the real thing now, not the misshapen and slimy creature of a distorted consciousness.

We've already seen how oppressive it can be to live always in a state of being forgiven, like a child constantly wrecking the furniture or the glassware. The operative word, of course, is "constant." We can feel ourselves caught in a relationship of never being sure when we'll be stepping on the sensitive nervous system of a perfect God.

God is always right, and I am always wrong, or never quite right, or at least never up to expectation. (Whose expectation, of course?) At some point I have to ask myself whether I'm willing to drop my expectations and accept his. But being willing may not be quite enough. His expectations can be so foreign to me, so elusive and confusing, that I cannot function in the kind of mental world they structure. God's expectations for me are rooted in the kind of forgiveness we've been talking about, and that is why we've been talking about it. We have to try, not only to walk around in the bewildering world made by a kind of forgiveness which is very unlike our understanding of the word, but also to try our limited best to grasp its nature. We cannot live continuously in the false kind of forgiveness our imaginations conjure up when the word is spoken. We can — to the extent of our ability to transcend that tortured imagination — live in relaxation and pleasure in the real thing. Or at the very least, we can recognize that our reactions to it are not to it, but to an emotional creation of our own.

For instance. Yes, we say, forgiveness is a form of love. The love does not diminish and increase according to what we consider our deserts. Its totality is not static, for the sea does not just lie there where the land gives way. Even its calmest sunlit surface is filled with passion and adventure. And returning to the symbol of plant life, a garden, at its quietest, never ceases to grow, never ceases to offer us its fragrance and its dappled light.

All right, forgiveness is love. But isn't this an inferior sort of love?

After all, we're the object of some kind of condescension, aren't we? There's nothing here of equality, is there? And therefore aren't our own small loves better proportioned to us? Or, more distressing still, can't we imagine (if our little loves have tossed us onto a compost heap of disillusion), a better love than that which we perceive under the name of mercy? Can't we dream up for ourselves a better love and, in consequence, a better God?

Certainly we can dream up a better sort of divine love than that which our tangled heads and hearts are in danger of coming up with — a better God as well. But that is not the same project as improving on the real thing.

And one characteristic of the real God is that he is the one who desires *us* more than we could ever want anything at all. "If I were not myself, but the handsomest, cleverest, and best man in the world, and were free," says Tolstoy's Pierre to Natasha, "I would this moment ask on my knees for your hand and your love!"[47]

This is really what God himself has done. His work of re-creation was not accomplished from above but from below. He knelt at our feet to wash our hearts; he sprawled in our streets and bled into our soil.

The catch here is that, to many of us, this eagerness to share our suffering and degradation is not an expression of an attractive love, but the ultimate reproach. Most of us know a few martyred spirits, the kind who live and suffer for others, letting these others know (head-on or sideways) that they are the cause of such well-borne affliction. It is no fun to be backed into the position of pain-giver, loaded with guilt, and favored with reproach unacknowledged by the reproacher. Spare us at all cost from that kind of love.

To make it worse, God is perfect; he has never hurt us. But we have a long record of hurting him. And we keep at it. To be always the one who needs forgiveness is not pleasant. How can you relate to someone you never cease hurting?

And why should we? After all, he's independent, he has everything. He doesn't need us. So isn't his love a kind of pity? And pity is okay, it's better than nothing, but it doesn't appeal as the end and goal of existence, as what a weary and very battered race is wading through its history to get to.

But someone who loves is not independent, not in that way. And God is not pitying or condescending or a reproachful victim. We cannot invent a more beautiful love than the one we are made to receive from him and to return in full measure. As a matter of fact, all our fairy-tale endings and romantic fantasies are only brief and fragile glimpses of the fulfillment we are meant to have in his eternal arms.

The fact is that many of our problems are rooted in our false apprehensions of our own worth, and in a defective style of coping with this. We can project onto God our hatred of ourselves, or find no one else so appropriate as he to blame for what we wish we weren't.

It can be hard to let go of all that stuff that goes with guilt, that makes us feel we're at home in the manure heap, and if we just stay here quietly we can't fall through and wind up in worse shape. Who wants to let go of the satisfaction which comes from feeling that "You, God, let me get into this mess of mediocrity. *I* had ideals and aspirations, and it's *your* fault I can't reach them. So why should I let you forgive me for being what I never wanted to be?"

We can even bark into the face of a forgiving God, "I hate you for my disappointment in myself, for setting up this system in which the answer is what I don't want it to be — forgiveness. I will hang on to my guilt as a kind of punishment to you for not letting me be better."

Much of this can be the effect of real guilt, and Speer knew all about that. And much, or some of it, can be entangled in an emotional guilt which has little relation to the real thing. A mother or father or someone else from the sensitive years of our growth is inside us, telling us we're no good, or we have to earn our worth in some way we know isn't possible. Our inner world is being run by someone, by that other, and to accept the garden and the love free for nothing is just about impossible. My place is the garbage can. It's where I belong; I've been told so.

Many of the disabilities which make our acceptance of forgiveness so difficult will be around for the rest of our lives. We need not smash our heads against them until our brain is dizzy and in pain. If we can mitigate their effects, we ought to. If they continue with us for the rest of our lives, we can take advantage of them for our spiritual good. The offering to God of our willingness to surrender an attachment to guilt can be a rich gift and a point of deep communion with him.

We pray, we carry, we try to laugh at the needs inside us which have formed the expectations that make us feel so ugly. We give him the self that does not want to be given, and we accept the forgiving love whose effect we do not feel.

At this point, we'd better construct a heap of our problems, rages, resentments, and misunderstandings of God and call in another image. It is my favorite symbolic representation of the human situation as lost and saved. If it didn't (as I remember) happen in a garden, it should have. And I refuse to consider another setting.

In the last scene of the 1950's film *An American in Paris,* Gene Kelly and Leslie Caron have parted. He stands at the top of a stone stairway in a park beside a Paris street. She returns to Maurice Chevalier, her fiance, who is waiting in a car by the curb below. The surprise is that Chevalier knows that Leslie is in love with Gene Kelly and lets her go. As Kelly watches, she opens the car door and begins to run *up* the steps toward him. He takes one look at her radiant face and runs *down* the steps toward her.

The camera pans from one face to the other. Each is luminous, eager, and transformed. An incredible love has been taken away and given back. And they run toward an embrace that is even less important than the movement that it gathers into itself.

This is the real picture of salvation; this is the reality of God's love for us and of its identity with his forgiveness.

Chapter 10

The Giving-In

When I first read the jacket of *Inside the Third Reich,* I felt that here was a man who had done the hardest thing we can ever be asked to do. He had, as I was to read in his own words, "laid waste" his moral life. He had given over his talents to the making of pain and destruction, and the fame he had so desperately sought had stuck to him in the form of a dense and reeking notoriety. Yet he found a reason for going on, and go on he did. In the ruins of his moral life, in a confrontation with the unspeakable damage which that life had inflicted on the world, he was able to live out an experience of genuine re-creation.

Few of us could have borne the weight of Albert Speer's repentance. But small-time dabblers in evil as we are, it is here, precisely here, at the crossroads of acceptance and forgiveness, that the lives of all of us find their meaning, and the gate swings open onto Paradise. Our virtue, such as it is, cannot force the lock. Our virtue is our glad response to the gift of mercy laid in a heart that has acknowledged its isolation, its self-interested ambition, its harshness, and its stunted growth.

And what are the effective results of this response, of this fresh flowering in the wilderness?

For one thing, we can begin to forgive others. Perhaps there is one other, or several, with whom in the very depths of our life history we have been bitterly entangled. This other can be God himself, parents or siblings, a spouse, friend, employer. The emotional fallout from such a negative relationship can be directing our entire mood system and infecting every reaction. Does moving into God's forgiveness automatically heal this destructive relationship? It might, but it probably won't do a complete job. The roots of such pain run deep, and — again — time is a favored tool of God: time and the learning of skills. A garden does not grow haphazardly. Cultivation is a craft, and so is integral forgiveness. But our bungling efforts struggle in a new strength: the grace of God's forgiving love. We begin.

Another aspect of our response can show in a spirit of thanksgiving and praise. A hurting heart brings up a harvest of complaint. It generates a thorny, overgrown wasteland that bloodies the hands of everyone with courage enough to touch it, and eventually finds itself alone, untouched and unwanted — if not enmeshed with someone else's thorns. The forgiven heart can start to notice the sunlight and welcome the rain, can grow at least a few more dandelions and a few less thistles. It need no longer live constantly on the gripe.

One of the finest effects of our willing to let ourselves rest in the embrace of divine forgiveness is just that: the ability — at least some of the time — to relax. We no longer see ourselves involved in a trade agreement with God: forgiveness in exchange for good behavior. Our efforts at conversion are not aimed at God's approval, his love and acceptance, forgiveness itself. They grow *from* these things. We are so grateful for the love that we can't just let it lie there. We have to let it grow into a garden: our own special, individual landscape, desired from all eternity and never to be duplicated.

And in this we see the fulfillment of our mission. Hitler is dead. Poverty, atrocity, torture, exploitation, human misery multiplied by uncountable millions are still around. Most of us have food, cleanliness, shelter, freedom, a magnificent cultural heritage.

We have no right to this unless we are playing our part, accepting our responsibility toward the whole world, the exploited and the exploiter. Going to church is not enough. Being reasonably polite to our brothers and sisters is not enough. Facing our responsibilities for social justice and the natural world is still not enough. Putting in the prayer even is not enough. All this, necessary and good as it is, is not the deepest reason for our being.

Giving ourselves to the growth process, to the work of conversion, is what we're here for and what makes all the rest count. Giving ourselves to forgiveness and restoration, we offer our own weakness and sin and, in it, that of the world, joyfully, lovingly.

We let the garden grow, haul the bricks, plant the iris, carry the watering cans, admire the gift of growth.

We have become animal lovers. I have even forbidden the others to chase mice in my part of the garden.[48]

May 7, 1960. Sunday. A blackbird bathed in the bathtub pond and afterward sang above my head in the walnut tree. A young sparrow lost its way underneath the garden bench. Meanwhile five hawks practiced stunt flying in the wind. One of them settled down on a water faucet a few meters away from me, flew onto the lawn to drink from the bathtub, and because it is still young and clumsy, almost fell over on its face. Finally a young wild pigeon came and perched on the lowest branch of the walnut tree, under which Hess and I had already been sitting for an hour in silence. Into the stillness Hess said, with almost a touch of embarrassment, "Like Paradise."

Will I later miss these quiet days with books and gardening, free from ambition and vexation? Sometimes I have the feeling that time is standing still. When did I come here? Have I always been here? In the evenness of the days, which simply flow by, time can fall into oblivion. Perhaps this was what life was like in the monasteries of the Middle Ages. Isolation not only from people, but also from the bustle of the world.

Sitting on the garden bench today, for a moment I saw myself as a monk, and the prison yard as the cloister garden. It seemed to me that my family alone still links me to the outside. Concern with everything else that makes up the world is more and more dropping away from me, and the idea of spending the rest of my days here is no longer

*frightening. On the contrary, there is great peacefulness in
the thought.*

*Is this submission a weakness or resignation? In any
case it makes things easier. The thought in fact has already occurred to me that it may be another, novel form of
dealing with my fate. After language studies, architecture
courses, book projects, and an around-the-world tour, it
may be the last and perhaps the wisest way to give meaning to my lot. It is a matter not of seizing fate by the
throat, to use Beethoven's famous phrase, but of willingly
putting oneself into its hand.*[49]

Part III

The Tools

Chapter 11

The Tools

Conversion is the most concrete expression of the working of love and of the presence of mercy in the human world.[50]

Though conversion is the blossoming of mercy and not a dogged attempt to deserve and control it, conversion still demands a lot of doing. We might or might not expect prison to provide someone with these spiritual landscaping tools. Spandau did. Because it was not Buchenwald, it was able to maintain life, and its disciplines acted, to the opened heart, much as the classical forms of spiritual ascesis.

Prison Asceticism

Take silence, for instance. Spandau offered Speer generous amounts of silence: conversation with his fellow inmates was usually less welcome than a quiet cell; and not all the guards were friendly. Or solitude. Speer had always been, to some extent, a solitary person; his addiction to work had hidden this, and his need to belong had revealed it, but not to him. Spandau, which intensified this loneliness, also made him painfully aware of it. Solitude would follow him out of prison and pervade the remaining years of his life. For whose experience could reach into the cave of his heart and give him the kind of understanding that might erase his radical loneliness?

Solitude and guilt gave a particularly poignant quality to what he called "the enforced celibacy of Spandau." For he had left his wife, Margarete, and their six children to struggle alone with their destiny as family of a convicted war criminal. And twenty years of imprisonment were to leave him in a spiritual and emotional world which continued to inhibit the expression of his genuine but perhaps crippled love for them. They were to remain strangers to this husband and father of such formidable experience.

> *Today a long letter from Hilde which alarmed me; it sounds very alienated. For a long time I have been unable to conjure up any image of her. No member of the family knows what it means to be imprisoned. They cannot imagine how much effort it costs me with every visit, every letter, not to depress them.*[51]

Surely this man knew poverty, dressed in regulation brown corduroy with his number stamped on the knees of the pants and the back of the jacket. He didn't have even a name: to the guards he was "Number Five." In face of this obliteration of individuality, the prisoners maintained some pretense of a social code by addressing one another as "Herr." And once when a visitor approached him as "Herr Speer," Number Five carried a dizzied ego back to his cell: "*Herr* Speer!"

Obedience? Well, if it was hardly enlightened monastic obedience, it served at least some of the functions of monastic obedience. He had stability surely, for he served his entire twenty years without leaving the prison property. Newspapers were eventually permitted, and gossip with the guards kept them informed of events outside, but the prisoners were maintained in an effective separation from the world. Without doubt, they had a regulated day, one whose structure he intensified for his own mental health.

> *I am beginning to set up a program for myself, to organize my life as a convict. To be sure, I have only the experience of six weeks to go by, with more than one thousand and thirty weeks still before me. But I already know that a life plan is important if I am to keep going.*[52]

His relationship with his cell should surprise no one, since the cell seems to capitulate the popular image of prison life:

My cell is 3 meters long and 2.7 meters wide.... As in Nuremberg, the glass of the window has been replaced by cloudy, brownish celluloid. But when I stand on my plain wooden stool and open the transom of the window, I see the top of an old acacia through the stout iron bars, and at night the stars.[53]

He had time for reflection:

It must be more than a matter of organizing sheer survival. This must also become a time of reckoning. If at the end, after these twenty years, I do not have an answer to the questions that preoccupy me now, this imprisonment will have been wasted for me. And yet I fully realize that even at best my conclusions can only be tentative.[54]

And plenty of time to read. I sometimes almost envied him his range of reading matter, and the time in which he lay on his cot, bundled up during winter in every article of clothing he had, reading and reading and reading. But more important than the time he spent at it, was the way in which he did it.

This morning I read in Goethe's Elective Affinities, *"Everything seems to be following its usual course because even in terrible moments, in which everything is at stake, people go on living as if nothing were happening." I used to read such sentences without noticing them. Now I associate them with my situation. In general I notice how my reading is becoming a kind of portentous commentary on my past. I haven't read this way since the end of my secondary-school days.*[55]

Now that is monastic. It's practically a lesson in how to do *lectio divina* — in an unusual text.

And though it would be hard to find a more deplorable example of community life than Spandau, the people with whom he lived made more than a fragile contribution to his spiritual regeneration in one way or another. Manual labor, as we have seen, became an indispensable element in his conversion.

His references to it can also be funny and sound like anyone's monastic experience.

> *Depending on the weather, I turn the soil or paint our corridor. I lay a board between two rickety ladders and balance on it two meters above the ground while the whitewash runs over my head and hands. It soon stops being fun, but I tell myself that this is a kind of balancing exercise for future hikes in the mountains. Every day I climb up and down the ladders perhaps a hundred times. A hundred times two meters makes an altitude of two hundred meters. A few days ago, when I was moving the ladders, a heavy hammer I had placed on top of one fell on my head. Four stitches needed to close the wound.*[56]

He had prayer.

The Goal and the Means

These are all recognizable ascetical tools. But many unrecognizable ones also gave formation to his life, as they do to ours. Humor, for instance, has to be a universal ascetical practice. Speer's diary, somber as it had to be, is also consistently hilarious. You laugh out loud. For Speer, humor was more than a survival mechanism. From our perspective we can see it as his holy and humble acceptance of human incongruity. Incidents which invited a whine or the crack of invective emerged as wry and even self-deprecating humor.

Conversation (such as it was), food and fast, service of others, the personal disciplines of survival which we will examine in a later chapter: these and many other almost unseen rituals of daily life made up one man's response to mercy, the response which we call conversion.

Chapter 12

The How of It

I have said that what Spandau offered Albert Speer were the traditional forms of ascetical practice, as well as a set of survival techniques universal enough but peculiarly adapted to his situation. The lot was rather bleak than otherwise, but there it was. And even though he could hardly be conscious of its transcendent function, it was going to do him spiritual service.

"Albert Speer, why have you come?"

"I have come to accept in myself the world's judgment on the Third Reich, to accept responsibility for my leadership. And to atone."

That is what he intended, and as far as it went, his intention was good. It would open the door of his heart to the work of these tools of the spiritual craft. And more, far more, would be achieved in him than he could have foreseen on July 19, 1947, or than he ever realized in this mortal life.

But how did these tools of the spiritual craft contribute to his regeneration? How do our similar ones contribute to ours? Obviously, on the one hand, they do so by supporting our efforts to embrace better values and to express these in our actions. Prayer, reading, silence and solitude, community, labor: we use these tools to mature our response. Though we may feel overstocked with advice on how to use them, the part played by successful use of our instruments is fairly straightforward and understandable. It's nice to be able to be virtuous when we want to be, especially when we — and others — have suffered a lot from our bad habits. What is not so understandable is the part played by failure. Why should the frustrations of our well-intentioned efforts do us so much good? Or even our spiritual failures?

For one thing, our desires for the wrong things get tangled in our desires for the right ones, and failure can untangle the snarls.

What Do You Want?

Yes, what do we want?

Each of us who enters an experience of conversion wants something good, something that is more important than anything else. Certainly we do not want ascetical practices, not for the sake of being ascetic. We learn to make friends with them because they will help us gain that other basic something which is so supremely important. Whatever the particular emphasis given by our personality and call, we want to fulfil our human vocation — or our vocation to be human.

What we have to be careful about is the twisted and quirky character of our motivation. We want God, and we want as well a lot of other things that conflict with wanting God.

Beneath my desire for God and for the well-being of other people, beneath my intellectual recognition of how salvation works and my sincere willingness to give myself to the saving fact of God, dwells a powerful and complex world of fear, ambition, pain, compensatory drives, and unenlightened instinct. I'm rather used to turning myself over to it, letting it form my expectations and set my goals.

This is why my best intentions can so easily become the servant of the disabilities they set out to heal. My use of what the *Rule of Benedict* calls the instruments of good works can quickly become instruments in service of the same old attitudes and behaviors they were meant to alter. Silence, for instance, can nurture an atmosphere of prayer. Or it can provide the mirror in which I keep checking out the spiritual persona in which my weak self-esteem is taking refuge. Or it can become the vehicle for a "legitimate" brush-off of someone I dislike.

Do I really want the self-revelation of God, or do I want

what I think it ought to feel like, or how it ought to work? Do I want to be a person more supple to the work of the Spirit, or do I want to be what I feel I have to be in order to make peace with myself? I want the will of God, or do I? Do I want instead to be what I myself have determined I have to be in order to please God?

I want prayer. Or do I? Do I want the prayer which transcends my emotional needs for a certain type of prayer? I want union with God. Or I do until the saving love of God chooses to work through the collapse of my attempts at union with God. I want community, but am I willing to sustain years of the pain of wounded self-images attacking one another? How do I survive when my own pretensions rub raw the thin skin of people who have learned to be obnoxious because they've been convinced for so long that they're no good?

I want to help the world. But can I accept the frustration of seeing that I'm not making a dent on the job to be done? When I find that the world will not conform to my ideas of how it ought to be reformed, do I realize that what I want is not the healing of the world, but its healing on the terms and by the method I lay down? Can I see that what I really want is the confirmation of my own ideas on how it ought to behave and be happy?

Why the Roof Falls In

Seeing that we have misused our tools and deformed our structures is a healthy step on the way. It's not something we can avoid by being careful and meaning well. It happens more often than we would like. The reaction can be panic, discouragement, paralysis. Or we can accept as a gift the fact that our tools have a double function: to carry us onward and to let us down. Both are good.

When we put our instruments into the power of our disabilities, the grand spiritual endeavor has to go smash at times, not because the structures don't work, but because they work so well. They destroy because they are faithful, to their nature and to ours. They are giving us the opportunity to offer our unreal expectations to the love that has been waiting for just this chance to attack them.

Even though we want to say, after one of these failures, "I hate my neighbor. I hate my neighbor's dog. My disposition is thirty times worse than when I began to get serious about God," despair is not a realistic response. The liturgy, the sacred reading, the daily rituals and struggles and constructive activities are still our spiritual friends, even though they seem to have grown teeth and claws. They have worked, but in their own way, by not working in the way we expected and demanded.

Their collapse has uncovered at least a little of what is underlying the "spiritual" expectations which have been disappointed. What the spiritual life wants of us is not a flawless performance, but the exposure of our inner selves in a saving conversation with God. We do not need the kind of virtue that protects us from salvation. And one function of the ascetic practices is to demolish this holy, protective wall.

Then when we have been invaded a little more deeply by the saving grace which let us smash up because it cared too much about us to let us remain all glued together, we can again take up these instruments with wiser, humbler, more practical hands. They welcome us back. They continue their teaching; they let themselves be used. But they continue to say as well, "Let yourself be taught — by defeat as well as by success, by failure as well as by achievement. Let's work together for the right kind of virtue: the kind that does not blame the past nor balk at the future, but accepts the now."

Now, with this faulty and beautiful self; with our misconceptions of what we're supposed to be doing and achieving; with what other people are here for and think they are here for; with how this particular system is supposed to work and doesn't always; with the responsibility to keep trying.

Now, with the past and what it has given in constructive elements and beautiful memories, weaknesses and guilt, the patterns of coping and reaction it has left, the residue of habitual choices, and the wisdom of experience.

Now, with our apprehensions of the future, our remaining unrealistic expectations, our despair and our hope.

Spandau was a release from bondage. It eroded the illusion of freedom, and opened the door to its reality. Our life too, whatever its *now* happens to be, can reveal our interior confinement and free us from it to a greater or lesser extent. The interesting part of it is that we often achieve this freedom precisely in the acceptance of our imprisonment, the inward and outward limitations and constrictions that will dissolve only in God's good time and that in our now, our meanwhile, are to be part of the saving drama of our lives.

The Acceptance of Our Imprisonment

But don't we get a new self after all this trouble? Here is this man spending twenty contrite years alone with God: didn't he get a new personality in exchange for the one he was so anxious to dump? No, he didn't. God took care of the essentials. The rest was something Speer and the people he related to — in and out of prison — had to put up with and attempt to handle as best they could.

We can want very badly to be someone else, or at least to be ourselves with a new set of inner equipment. Actually, we can determine on a kind of emotional suicide. We mean so well. Why can't we simply eliminate these habits of manipulation, defensive anger, self-obsession? Why can't we turn into a nice person who would deserve our own approval, and therefore the approval of God and of all these people out there whom we so want to impress?

The Rule of Benedict advises the abbot always to temper justice with mercy, "lest in seeking to scrape away the rust, the vessel itself be broken." Maybe we should be that kind of abbot to ourselves. The behavior we see as negative is emerging from an inner source of constructive as well as destructive action. We can't eliminate every negative manifestation of who we are without destroying the person we are. Unlike God, we do not come with the ability to create from nothing.

Jung has some wonderful, commonsense lines about the problems of life and of the self: they don't go away, and they're never completely solved. Our life project is not to make ourselves over from scratch but to keep on dealing patiently with what we're stuck with.

It's not a matter of ceasing to try, but of handling as serenely as possible the breakage and remending of our tools. Sometimes we question a conversion because the person who has gone through such a radical change is still imperfect. Albert Speer had what we all have: character faults. They didn't evaporate with his conversion, and why should they? He was, interiorly, an abandoned child with the aggressive and managerial faculties that go with the kind of gifts he had. His personal world was shadowed by the consciousness of terrible moral failure. No one should be surprised when, in such a man, a sense of shame, guilt, and inadequacy alternates with a drive to overcompensate. It's ridiculous to pour every motivation through a sieve in hope of finding something with which to denigrate his honesty or spiritual stature. Who among us could survive that sieve?

I want to say, "Let him have his character faults in peace." A lot he probably couldn't do. God and his response achieved the essentials. What was not essential, he was left to struggle with, and the struggle became part of his ongoing conversion.

Holiness is an acceptance of being filled with the holiness of God, and it's perfectly compatible with a wounded and flawed personality. In fact, the wounds and the flaws can open us to God. Holiness is not a state of never needing to be forgiven.

In the description of Hitler as he showed himself to me and to others, a good many likable traits will appear. He may seem to be a man capable and devoted in many respects. But the more I wrote, the more I felt that these were only superficial traits.

For such impressions are countered by one unforgettable experience: The Nuremberg Trial. I shall never forget the account of a Jewish family going to their deaths: the husband with his wife and children on the way to die are before my eyes to this day.

In Nuremberg I was sentenced to twenty years imprisonment. The military tribunal may have been faulty in summing up history, but it attempted to apportion guilt. The penalty, however poorly such penalties measure historical responsibility, ended my civil existence. But that scene had already laid waste to my life. It has outlasted the verdict of the court.[57]

Part IV

The Women

Chapter 13

From Afar

It's no fun, of course, when so much of conversion turns out to be radically other than getting something done, when our tools break and our strength ebbs out and our best intentions twist back on themselves and feed on their own substance. For the purpose of reflecting on this phase of our response, we could hardly do better than study Mark's treatment of the women at the cross.

> There were also women looking on from a distance, among whom were Mary Magdalen, and Mary the mother of James the younger and of Joses and Salome. These used to follow him and provided for him when he was in Galilee; and there were many other women who had come up with him to Jerusalem. (Mark 15:40–41)

The Waiting Women

Mark waits until after Jesus' death before calling attention to the waiting women. They had been there all along, but that is not Mark's point. Since they will be witnesses to the empty tomb, he must emphasize their witness to Jesus' death and entombment. Still, how did they get there in the first place? Studying Mark's account, we notice an interesting succession of verbs. First, in Galilee, they "followed" Jesus. This is a technical word which alerts us, if we didn't already know it, to the identification of these women with Mark's congregation, and with us; for it is we who are the followers. "Follow" is also an active, do-something kind of word. You tramp from village to village, hot, dusty, and harassed. You're hassled by

103

crowds and deafened by demanding voices, and after a few days you wonder whether there's an inconspicuous way to go home.

The miracles have become commonplace, and what you would really like are thinner crowds and going to bed on time. However, you didn't come to sight-see, and what you came for doesn't stop. You came to "serve" (or minister to or provide for, depending on your translation): another technical term, and another active job. Everyone else is tired too, and dirty, and above all, hungry. Everyone else needs somebody to put order into meal time (when there is mealtime) and wash clothes and keep the itinerant organization from falling apart. So you serve.

The end of it is not what you would have chosen. You "go up" with him to Jerusalem. Still on your feet, still following, you climb to the high, holy sanctuary. And then your function shifts. The verbs tell us what is happening.

You "look on." No longer walking, no longer cooking or washing or bossing people around, you stand still and watch. This is where the following has led you. He's not going anywhere and neither are you. But he *is* doing something, and your purpose is to help him do it. Yes, he is saving the world, but he is doing even more. He is revealing the nature of God and the nature of creation; he is showing you who you are and what you're for, and you are asked to be quiet and let yourself be shown. God has stripped himself naked, and he is silently explaining the intricate connections between himself and this creature he drew out of the earth and has loved and suffered from and is saving.

You learn, not by sweating but by keeping quiet, not by figuring things out (who, after all, could figure this out?) but by sharing, participating in what he is doing. You are no longer separate as the follower, but a sharer in his life and going forth. His life and death are entering you through your stricken eyes, and you are all of humanity, rooted to the earth from which you came, a million and a half years ago. You learn by being, by being one with, and by not running away. Let it in. Let the

Godhood in, all that you can hold; let all the why of human-kind come in, and agree to it. You are being instructed, as you are being saved.

One more significant word — or two in Greek as in English — has been slipped into the account. It is not a verb this time: "from afar," (or as here, "from a distance"). "From afar" can mean any number of things: left out, peripheral, unimportant, inactive, shoved aside. You aren't, as they say, where the action is. And that is because you're being called into a more radical kind of action — the action of passivity.

What a terrible word. You watch him die without being able to change anything or do anything. You watch the men of your company retrieve his body from the nails. You move your weary legs a few yards beyond the hill of sacrifice until you are again rooted, "sitting on" before the tomb — another verb, not of activity but of receptivity. You watch. You witness, you are sure of death.

Then you go home to keep the Sabbath. The sun, the unreliable sun of such a murky afternoon, goes down into hell. You rest as God is resting. The whole great labor is done. And the greatest labor lies in the greatest simplicity: that of accepting the Seventh Day.

Then, " . . . very early in the morning after the Sabbath, they went to the sepulchre at sunrise, alleluia!"[58]

You have thought that, at least now, something can be *done*. At least now you can take your spices and anoint the body. But when you get there, you find no body to anoint. Your services are still not needed; they rest heavy in your hands. The tomb is empty.

St. Bernard catches it well when he says that the women who went to anoint Jesus' body were themselves anointed with the fragrant tidings of his resurrection. At this point, Mark differs from Luke and Matthew. His women say nothing: they are representing the members of Mark's congregation (and us) who wrap their wonder in blankets of social acceptance, and pretend, as Peter had, that they do not know the man. Luke and Matthew join John here to portray the proclamation of Easter;

the women tell the good news. But this is not until they have remained the appointed time in a state of being told.

The Passive

I said of the word "passive" that it was terrible.

A fence is passive to the brush which is slapping paint onto its surface. An anesthetized patient is passive to the surgeon's skill. A pregnant woman is passive to the process of gestation: she cannot hurry the development of her child. At a certain point in the progress of an addiction, its victim is truly a victim, and passive to its physiological laws.

With connotations like this, the word needs clarification. We could begin by discarding a number of misleading synonyms, words like "flaccid," "inert," "static," "stagnant," "languid" — and "dead." We could even drop the class of nice ones that indicate serenity: "tranquil," "unruffled," "calm," "hushed," "quiescent." What we're left with isn't much, because what we're left with is a confusing reality whose labels are all wrong. What would you find at the source of activity? Choice and energy. What would you find at the source of passivity, the kind I'm talking about? Choice and — though it seems in much lower supply — energy. Then what's the difference?

The difference, it seems to me, is this: an experience of activity emphasizes what we do. We exert ourselves in the interests of getting a handle on what's happening. We may succeed or we may not, but there's stuff upon which to exert our doing skills.

A passive experience, on the other hand, emphasizes what we can't do. Our opportunity for controlling, fixing, building, doing, is lessened, sometimes radically. Choice, in this case, endures, perseveres, gets on with it, sticks with it. Choice here is patient, sometimes resilient, obeying, groping, getting up in the morning to put one foot in front of another. Choice here summons up its courage and hope in face of the thing that cannot be done.

What is it then that we choose in agreeing to a set of circumstances, or what may seem to be a chaos of noncircumstance, which we cannot bind or mold or fashion?

We choose to accept the forming work of God — in ourselves and in whatever has been taken out of our own forming hands by his. God may not need or want the form of action we have determined to give; he may not want or give the result we've determined to have. We can choose to fight God's view of things, or we can choose to choose his vision and intent.

But, we argue, is God not working in our work, in our accomplishment, and in the growth attendant on all we can and should be doing? To do is human and God permeates the truly human in grace and goodness; he makes within our making. And we are accountable for all we should have done and haven't.

Of course. But God forms creation in more ways than one; the human heart has need of more than one form of making. And so we have to learn to wait. We have to learn to hold and give the waiting heart.

Chapter 14

Reversing Goals

What then of Speer? It's not surprising that once Albert Speer retrieved his conscience, his power of choice would operate in its usual mode — but with a new goal. He had been a man of action; he continued so. From his prison cell he could look back on this response to the light, an active resistance to Hitler, the man with whose ambitions his own had been so desperately identified.

He had driven on bomb-haunted roads, phoning as long as he had lines, persuading, "interpreting." He had played dangerous games with Hitler's volatility, planned even to kill him, and still managed to keep a power base from which to block the Fuehrer's terrible orders. Reversing goals but not means, he had remained the technocrat, the man who could handle any situation — until there was nothing left to handle, nothing to do except nothing. If he was to call the Nuremberg Trial the greatest act of psychic courage he had ever performed, it was also the first great experience of passivity he had ever known. His active choice to accept full responsibility for the war and its consequences was expressed in the refusal to defend his indefensible guilt.

This was a bright, taut moment which was to extend into the next twenty years, indeed into the rest of his life.

Prison: The Active Side

Speer did not walk into Spandau, turn off his head, and finish out his sentence in robotic acquiescence. I have talked about tools of the spiritual craft and mentioned other tools: instruments of physical and psychic survival. Surviving Spandau had to be a project, and he turned his mind to it as he had to every other problem in his life. He began as usual, actively.

Knowing he had to work, to organize his time and his mind in order to leave prison a whole man, he set out to maintain physical and mental health. First, there was the future to think about. He would keep up with developments in architecture:

> *I encourage myself with the thought that sometime in the future I shall be able to start over again from the beginning. More and more I have been considering how I can systematically deal with these years. I must work out a therapy, so to speak, in order to get through these nineteen years.*
>
> *My point of departure is that I must do the full twenty years. That means I shall leave here a man of sixty. At that age other men are thinking of retirement. Perhaps I shall then have ten years left...I am and shall remain an architect....If after these twenty years I still want to do something significant, I shall have to start where I left off in 1933....My old teacher Tessenow's idea of simple and human building has acquired a wholly new meaning for me, and for these times....As his former assistant and favorite disciple it is up to me to carry on his work. It's high time I had done with all these fits of melancholia over the grandiose plans, the unbuilt palaces and triumphal arches; high time for me to find my way back to my beginnings. Why shouldn't I be able to do something about housing for miners and applying my mind to the rebuilding of cities? It all depends on my managing to keep in touch with my profession.[59]*

He kept up with professional literature, began a study of the architectural history of the window, settled on a plan of regular walking, and took up gardening.

But he had more to deal with than the future. To this man, the past was a more severe form of prison than the bars of Spandau. He had to come to some kind of terms with that also. And so he kept a journal and began in secret to write his memoirs:

> *I have...realized how important writing is for this confrontation with myself. What has been written down, formulated with some care, takes on a certain stamp of definiteness.*[60]

He read with a settled plan, giving to his mind and conscience material from which to construct an explanation. The prisoners had access to Berlin's Central Library, excepting only works of a political nature. His program was impressive: art, drama, literature, philosophy, theology, history, cultural history, languages, geography. Perhaps sometimes he drugged himself with books, but at least as often they fed his search for light as they fed his thought. And he thought a great deal.

What about the present? Who can so devote himself to the past and the future as to obliterate his present? Who could spend so much time thinking, and thinking about the forty years he had used so badly, without trying to justify his present condition?

Imprisonment was important to Speer: imprisonment and punishment gave some moral shape to his life. His punishment was, he felt, setting a precedent, contributing to a juridical standard against which to measure the kind of crime for which he had accepted his sentence.

> *The conviction that my sentence is "unjust" because "the others" are making the same mistake would make me more unhappy than the sentence itself. For then there would be no hope for a civilized world. Despite all the mistakes, the Nuremberg Trial was a step in the direction of recivilization. And if my twenty years of imprisonment could help the German prisoners of war to get home only one month earlier, it would be justified.*[61]

> *It is hardly possible to convict us for violation of the Geneva Convention and at the same time hold millions of [German] prisoners of war for forced labor.*[62]

The hope that Nuremberg would make a tangible difference in world politics turned out to be naive, and the pain this caused him was intense. He was forced to find meaning on a deeper level, and, as we shall see later, he came to view his imprisonment itself as an assertion of responsibility in the ruins of a misdirected life. Just punishment is a proclamation of human dignity in the moral structure of society. His prison years were to be an active and constant pursuit of this value.

Prison: The Passive Side

The Rule of Benedict speaks of sharing now by patience in the sufferings of Christ, so as to enter into his glory. "Patience" is another of the unpleasant words whose root gives us the word "passive." Patience, to Speer, came to be linked to another of the "pass" words: "passage" — the passage of time. The function of time becomes all too apparent as his diary entries move through years of it. Any fool can bear a burden for a little while. It's the long haul that gets you down.

He did not move wholly from the active into the passive state. But his activity, which he never suspended, took on a different character. It spent much of itself in supporting him during a passive experience. It was infused by this kind of experience and tempered by it. Then also, the importance of the active decreased in proportion to that of the passive.

This happened in several ways.

The world of Spandau moved in on his active plans and often sent them sprawling.

His past was no light burden, the pain of guilt and of failed hopes. His present worked him over daily with humiliation, confinement, and monotony. He who had lived for status had become "Number Five," dependent on the kindness of guards who were friendly, subject to the acrimony of others who were not, and to the petty intrigues of his fellow inmates. Day after day offered temptations to self-pity, self-excuse, and despair.

The future? That had to be let go:

I realize that all my efforts, all my interest, were directed less to the present than to the past and the future. It has all along been confrontation with the former, preparation for the latter....But isn't this here my real life?...I shall leave this prison an old man. What's all this about a new beginning?...An old man out of days long past turns up again, an embarrassment to neighbors and friends....I am acting as though a life still lies before me and this is only an interlude. But this cell, that wretched rock garden, my bean experiments and jokes with the guards, are all that is left to me. Beyond that what awaits me is merely a kind of epilogue.[63]

In earlier years I was scarcely able to conceive how Charles V at the height of his power could renounce the world and choose an existence as a monk. Today that thought is more familiar to me than any other....Will I still be able to cope with the world? Or instead will I cry out like that Pope Celestine whom they fetched from a hermit's cell and brought to Rome, "Give me back my desert!"[64]

He recognized the slowly eroding effects of what Hopkins calls "the world without event":

There remains a curious feeling of emptiness, as though these years had not existed.[65]

I would always have thought that a prisoner's real unhappiness lay in the loss of freedom, in being at the mercy of inferiors who serve as guards, in the constant sense of one's helplessness. It now surprises me that the outer as well as the inner lack of event is the real source of despair. Protected by a certain aloofness, one is ultimately actually grateful for the harassment of guards; for this heightens the feelings and at least creates the possibility of events...I observe how necessary man's emotions are to him....

The monotony of the past weeks has been wiped away; once again there are other things besides getting up, breakfast, cleaning cells, garden work, walk, and so on until sleep — the eternal, unchanging round.... This Cuban crisis, which is threatening the very life of the world, provides a certain element of life for us. Of course we are also extremely upset by the confrontation. But our very nervousness gives us a center of gravity.[66]

Driven deeply inward by confinement, by the denial of expansion, this least introspective of men grew into a sensitive and subtle observer of his own inner life and continued what he had begun: the honesty to confess what he saw. The man of technology was slowly growing into a man of the spirit, passing from hubris into humility. The master of the mechanical was coming to realize that what matters most is a simple act of human kindness. Time was destroying his own goals and achieving God's instead.

Chapter 15

The Women

The waiting heart — yes, it was Speer's own, as we will see; but it was also the inner world of the women whose lives were affected in some way by the choices he made and the person he was. "Afar off," or perhaps even more sharply, "at a distance," is also descriptive of their position by the cross of his own solitude.

Women have traditionally known much of the waiting factors in life. I am not praising a cultural situation which demeans and exploits the woman. I do praise the inner spirit of a woman who can make of emotional and material limitation a tutor of humanity and grace. What cannot be changed can be exploited in its turn for the sake of human growth. It can be, it has been — but not always. Injustice, yes, but also the unavoidable tangles of human relationships can embitter and confuse.

Something in this history of woman has expressed a truth about the human situation, even when this truth was harshly or unjustly forced out. It is the truth about our need for waiting, for living out time in which we have minimal control of circumstance.

Somebody has to wait. Someone has to symbolize whatever it is in all of us which must yield to a degree of passivity, frustration, insecurity, emptiness. And by this I do not mean a romantic sort of emptiness, but the painful absence of something we need. I am talking about that in us which has to let go of fashioning ourselves and our world, which has to live out the Sabbath mode of existence in a proportion more or less great. We still need the old story of Penelope, who represents a reality in the spiritual life of men as well as of women. We learn from the pain of Albert Speer's wife, Margarete, and his daughter Hilde, his loyal secretary, Annemarie. And even the tragedy of Eva Braun can teach.

Three of them knew the particularly anguished form of waiting which attends a relationship into which we just don't fit, the deeply frustrating experience of loving when the other can't love back in the manner we want so terribly.

This waiting demands the giving up of the kind of relationship one is most determined to have. The pattern is familiar. Once the difficulties show, and tears or shouting or withdrawal do not help, bitterness takes over. Whatever in us needs this man — as husband, father, son, or friend — agrees to pain or rebels against it. Either we grow beyond our expectations and find peace in a new dimension of love, or we move on into cynicism, a danger to ourselves and everyone else.

In this case, if the life beyond this one, the life for which we reserve the wholly inadequate name of heaven, is less than a vivid promise, the bewildered heart goes on in overt or repressed hostility. It suffers from any of the variations which deprivation plays on the emotional system, and something within dies. This earthly life cannot give the fruition one has determined on, and the next appears too nebulous to moderate the emotional distress.

Perception alters too. We see this other, this person once so all-important, through the filters of our disappointment, inadequate to our needs. More painful still, we can realize — and sometimes not realize — that the other is capable of a growth and relationship that can be evoked only by others, not by those who most need and want to be the instruments of deliverance and the receivers of a liberated love. Other people, other experiences, can reach, touch, and bring to life a person we will never know. And that's no fun at all.

Margarete

Some marriages are good, or good enough. Some marriages are violently bad, some go sour quietly. Some maintain a constant tension in which each partner wants of the other what the other cannot give. Speer's marriage was not good. The Hitler years, the prison years destroyed what seems to have been a fairly fragile beginning. Ironically, the experience of Hitler, which broke Speer open to repentance and a profound spiritual journey, also wrecked his chances for a placid, conventionally happy marriage.

> *I am going to need a good deal of courage to survive the twenty years. But will it not be even harder to face my family and my children? Will it not take still more courage to answer their questions when they come to visit me now or later and want to know how I could have participated in a regime that the entire world feared and despised? They will imply that they will always remain the children of a war criminal. And my wife's courage when she sits facing me and does not say that the ten years just past did not belong to her but to Hitler, and the twenty years that lie before us likewise. And finally, the courage to settle with myself the meaning of the past and my share in it.*[67]

In his active years he virtually abandoned her. His prison experience she could not share. In fact he felt he had to conceal his pain from her lest in breaking down entirely he intensify her own distress.

> *Perhaps I'll postpone my wife's next trip until August; then we'll be able to have ¾ of an hour. With short half-hour visits we are all worked up during the first quarter hour at seeing each other again, and during the second at having to say goodbye.*[68]

> *My wife's visit has once again thrown everything into turmoil. Her presence makes me realize that it was not only I who was sentenced in Nuremberg, but she also. It is hard to say which of us suffers more. For days after such a visit I am in no condition to talk with anyone; I go about alone with myself and my thoughts.*[69]

How do you relate to the husband whom you see for an hour four times a year with four or five guards listening in? How do you relate to him after his release, after forty years of being locked out of his world of experience? She knew no way of doing this. He took the blame he knew he deserved for choosing to walk away from her so many years before. But he had been in some other place for so long that emotionally he could not come back. He had taken another road, and when their paths converged again, he was someone she couldn't know, someone she couldn't make into the kind of man she had waited for. She expected someone else to walk out of Spandau, and that someone was no longer there, if he had ever been.

It was hard for her to understand his need for a certain amount of solitude in which to regain his balance. In an attempt to share this unreachable life, she filled his space and invaded his legitimate privacy. His spiritual life was shut away from her, for she had not shared its formation. This stranger was not the man she wanted, and when her struggles to make him so did not succeed, each partner suffered from the other — she in bitterness and he in guilt. When at last someone else walked into his loneliness, although I can't defend it, I can understand.

Everything in this earthly life does not work out.

Hilde

Women must too often rear their children alone, and Margarete's situation was particularly delicate, for the father of her six children was a convicted war criminal. How do you teach young children who need to love and admire their father that he is indeed worthy of admiration, this man they occasionally see behind a grate under surveillance? How do you put into young minds and characters the wisdom to recognize repentance as a key to the mystery of love, growth, suffering, and life — and see it as something we all share? How do you help them to confront the sore and shaming place within themselves where their father ought to be, when you yourself resent your own experience of him, and when he is not able to be the only kind of father you can want for them? She was a loved and loving mother, but her own bitterness complicated their already difficult relationship with a recovered father.

Hilde was his older daughter. Her cheerful visits to Spandau bring a sigh of relief to the reader of the diaries, and she shared a long correspondence with him. But she also found herself between a rock and a hard place. The active form of her love expressed itself in persistent efforts to obtain her father's earlier release. Her failure at every approach to authority was only one form of passivity.

> *Perhaps I can forgive myself for everything else.... But I have absolutely nothing to say for myself when a name like Eichmann's is mentioned. I shall never be able to get over having served in a leading position a regime whose true energies were devoted to an extermination program. How can I make that clear to anyone? ... How would I be able to explain it to my wife? To my daughter Hilde, who with all the ardor of her twenty years writes letters and appeals, tries to mobilize sympathy, goes to see people, and tries to obtain intervention, in order to free her father. Will they ever be able to understand that I want to get out of here and yet see a meaning in my being here?*[70]

More serious was her own inability to reach and love and admire this man she needed and must have wanted to love. I have always wondered at the force that drives a child's need for parental love, and for not one parent alone, but for whatever both have to give. To lose one, and to lose him in these circumstances must have been a serious deprivation. I often wonder what that place within her grew to be, the place where he should have been and wasn't, or where there lived a partial and distorted image of his true self.

To her, possibly most of all, it would have been a source of comfort to recognize the privileged nature of the converted heart. She could then have related to her father without the destructive emotional barrier of perceiving in him a guilt she could not recognize as transformed and transforming, a glory instead of the constant specter of his moral inferiority.

Annemarie Kempf

Sometimes a stereotype can surprise us, turning toward us the most beguiling face and a unique human story. Then we realize it's not a stereotype after all. Almost from the beginning of his career with Hitler, Annemarie Kempf acted as Albert Speer's secretary. The relationship was not a sexual liaison, and never did she languish from frustrated romantic attachment. She did not sacrifice her buoyantly independent personality to the adoration — clear-eyed as it was — in which she held him. He was, quite simply, her life.

She moved to Nuremberg to be near him during the trial and to assist in providing documentation. During his imprisonment, she coordinated efforts to secure his release, while continuing a new vocation, her work with disabled children. She maintained this mission until her death, and he assisted it financially from his publishing royalties.

Her vocation to waiting grew not only from her inability to be of active help to him in his prison years, but also and even primarily from her highly empathetic participation in his own suffering. During Spandau, after Spandau, she carried along with him his inconsolable pain.

One day during his imprisonment, while casually seated on the floor conversing with a friend, another woman pressed her, against her protests, to talk about Spandau. Annemarie began to laugh nervously, then crumpled to the floor in anguished sobs. Speer was serving his sentence in one way, and she in hers.

Though he had to appreciate her faithfulness, it is doubtful that Speer was ever able to conceive what a totality of love had been given him in her. The beauty of it was that in Annemarie, the love bore such abundant fruit, and the participation in another's helplessness deepened her capacity to heal and serve a wider circle of the dispossessed.

Eva Braun

We could even add Hitler's loyal little mistress to the list. Shy and self-conscious about her position, she was hard to know, hard to be a friend of — and she seems to have had very few beyond Speer, who became her confidant. Simple, unsophisticated, unassuming, and probably not very intelligent, she is the most pathetic character in his story. Yet in her, Speer recognized qualities of character that other people missed. He befriended her from compassion; but more than that, he respected her, as Hitler did not.

Of all the ways in which she could have thrown away the precious gift of her life, the way she chose seems the most entirely tragic — wasting those years of waiting, of loving, of boredom and emptiness, on a man with so little capacity for response.

> *We were able to talk honestly, for Hitler had withdrawn. She was the only prominent candidate for death in this bunker who displayed an admirable and superior composure. While all the others were abnormal... Eva Braun radiated an almost gay serenity. "How about a bottle of champagne for our farewell? And some sweets? I'm sure you haven't eaten in a long time." I was touched by her concern; she was the first person to think that I might be hungry after my many hours in the bunker.... She was also the only person in the bunker capable of humane considerations. "Why do so many more people have to be killed?" she asked. "And it's all for nothing...."* [71]

I hope God made up to her for all that was confused and foolish in her system of choices. I hope that her emptiness is filled now and that she is safe and at home.

Chapter 16

The World without Event

Yet God (that hews mountain and continent,
Earth, all, out; who with trickling increment,
   Veins violets and tall trees makes more and more)
   Could crown career with conquest while there went
Those years and years by of world without event
That in Majorca Alfonso watched the door.

          —Gerard Manley Hopkins, "St. Alphonsus Rodriguez"

Strange, how busy can be a world without event, how full of things to do. Have you ever taken a sheep by the wool of its back? Sheep are easily unsettled emotionally, and the touch will set them running. Their little feet pound the earth, their legs race off to nowhere, since you're hanging on to their wool. "Now, Sheep," you say, "calm down." But it takes time. It can take awhile for us too sometimes to realize we aren't going anywhere. Activity is not always activity. Sometimes it is the mindless thumping of hooves, the piston motion of legs with no destination. We have to calm down and look around.

Is something happening that we can't dominate or shape? Are we being held by circumstance, and if we are, have we chosen a way to deal with it, or have our instincts, our disordered fears and ambitions taken over our reactions to an exterior situation we can't change?

Insignificance

"Insignificance," like "passivity," is not a welcome word. In fact, it's downright frightening. We get a sheepy reaction, as if

this were the threat from which we have spent a lifetime running. Is that what we're born for? Is that what we learned a
craft or chose a profession for, got married and reared children
for? Move over, sheep, you have a point.

Nobody wants to be insignificant. We may think we know all
the reasons for our life choices: job, marriage, single or monastic state, volunteer work, charitable donations. To a degree we
do. And to a degree, in all those major turns of the road from
birth to death, an alert ear can hear the thump of running
hooves. We are racing from the threat of insignificance. Even
the fear of death is fear of a hand caught in the wool: I will
not have mattered, my life will disappear. There is, I think, only
one way to stop those thudding hooves. And that is to turn and
stand and face the threat, turn and face the passive periods of
life, the waiting, the seeming insignificance.

Although it can be hard to believe, our lives at these times
are, in fact, opening on a greater degree of development. We
are being asked to learn and to do in an even richer and more
radical way. Our hearts are held in hands which can accomplish
our destiny only when we have given them the freedom to do a
work we cannot do in any way other than by choosing to let it
be done in us.

What we can't do is often more important than what we can
do, and the activity which pulses within the confining arms of
an impossible situation is often the most expansive form of activity we will ever learn. Nobody asked us the first time if we
wanted to be born, but we are being asked again and again
to embrace new moments of birth. There are times when getting things done, even good, worthy, and totally constructive
things, is not enough. Waiting is what we're asked for, and only
waiting will do.

The inescapable fact is that to be fully human we must also
be more than human. And to give over to the action of a transcendent other the inner wells of our humanity is to act most
completely.

If only it felt that way.

The Waiting

You know what happens when something on which we relied for status or affection or some other kind of basic orientation gets pulled out from under our psychic system. We may still be overworked, but there's a humbling lack of distinction in our experience of self. No matter how faithful we are — to friend or family, to commitments and ideals — we find that we are living the fidelity of waiting for something we can't achieve. And that is often all we feel — that we aren't achieving.

In reality, God is saying to the stalled sheep in us, "Listen, receive. Take what I want to give you. Let me come as close as I want to. I know you want to be good. Do you also want to give me permission to love you with a kind of love you have not yet learned to imagine?"

Self-knowledge leads to this, prepares for this. But self-knowledge is the light in which the work is done, the light of a bright Christ who has come too close to let the darkness remain. It doesn't of itself do the work of change. And the work of change will require, at least at some point, the giving of ourselves to some hidden and inward thing being done to us, being born in us. Some time or other, we'll have to sit still.

"Still point" sounds romantic and unbothered. It's not really like that. This place can be a region of great uneasiness, of ragged temper, and a sense of everything being wrong. We feel pulverized and disconnected, and our very being is a reaching out for something to do, something to change, something, anything — just to get ourselves unsuffocated.

All sorts of personal difficulties will do the job of introduction, some to the point of daily anguish: all those ways in which we can't fix the world or save another person in our own way. But we have as well a good number of more ordinary passive experiences whose common quality disguises their function and true saving identity.

The Routine

The daily routine is one of these things. Some people collapse under the burden of sameness. They need the stimulus of variety or hovering deadlines or overwork. It's hard for them to hear, in a repetitive environment, the voice that whispers, "Look, you aren't being dumped into a machine in the morning and spit out at night. Let yourself be taught, taught by the common rhythm of the day, by time itself, by your own reactions to being cast up on the shore of routine, beached and flopping like a fish. Pay attention to the sacramental quality of common meals, the sacramental dignity of your own rhythmic nature."

We want, as we too well know, to take over. Oddly, the routine has as one of its functions to maintain in us some degree of this spirit of passivity.

Monastic Symbols

The great monastic practices are not a set of strange behaviors confined to people who don't live an ordinary life. They are particular *ways* of living out universal values in what is essentially a perfectly ordinary life. People living in other ways should be able to identify with these values and say: "Yes, I see. I want the essence of this thing myself. The same great truths are at the center of your life-style and mine, the same great ways of meeting human needs." We have seen this already with Speer.

And one of these great values is the one we've been talking about at this point in his development: the need to turn and face the threat of insignificance, of meaninglessness, the need to find ways of trying to stop the churning little legs within, the need to wait.

Obedience

Obedience, for instance, seems so specifically monastic. And yet, what is it but a sacrament of human limitation, of the human condition being opened onto infinity? Monastic obedience requires a lot of maturity, initiative, teamwork, and self-knowledge. It's not a way of throwing out our hard-earned skills of decision-making and the acceptance of responsibility. I have to say this, especially when we're anywhere near the context of the Third Reich. Mindless obedience was everyone's excuse at that time: "We did what we were told." Atrocities were someone else's fault. That is not the kind of obedience I'm talking about, but one that works within a well-formed conscience.

You would be surprised at the common elements which form the fabric of most monastic practices, including this one. We obey the particular assignments and customs which grow from a field of common need; so do most people of conscience. We cooperate in a common task, accept the network of what-cannot-be-changed, and attempt the changeables with what we hope is humor and tact. In what ways do I hold out the arms of my obedience to the love which waits beyond my own initiatives? In the limitations of my own personality, the effects on my community of its history and cultural environment, in the unchangeable aspects of other personalities and in God's timetable for their growth, in a situation of stress or conflict which has no apparent and certainly no immediate resolution. People whose vocation is other than monastic do this too, challenged by factors in their lives which no amount of anything but acceptance can handle. I think that most of the time each of us has to summon all our human wisdom and a lifetime of skills just to cope with the day's allotment of obedience.

And yet the symbolism of monastic obedience does not lie in how sensible it seems. The world is not always sensible, and a sacrament of the human condition has a great deal to tell us — all of which cannot be practical, logical, and tidy. What then is it saying?

Think of the illimitable God taking on limits, of the infinite Word speaking a human language, of eternity bound and bordered and surrounded by human obtuseness, weakness, and rebellion. Or on the other hand consider that the God for

whom daisies and walruses were an everyday creative enterprise could suddenly watch the lilies grow with eyes that employ
the common miracles of optics and the delicate wonders of a
human brain.

He chose, and in a way that is not open to us, both to receive
and to accept his manhood. By our obedience, by actively setting our power of choice in a human situation given to us, we
ratify and accept the fact of being this particular person in these
particular circumstances at this particular time. We accept what
it means to be human.

Yes, we hone and put to use the tools we are given. Yes, we
try to accomplish, to mold and improve and create the world to
which we have access. But our power of improvement is limited.
And monastic obedience speaks to those frontier situations, sec-
ular and sacred, in which choice appears to have come to the
end of itself and stands, seemingly left with only the willingness
to sacrifice opportunity, and yet knows that there we are not
less human or less creative.

Children are asked to do what they are told because they
don't know yet how to decide for themselves, and it is hoped
that they will catch on eventually to the reason behind the act.
Before they enter a monastery, monks have spent many years
learning to decide for themselves. And part of monastic obedience is just a continuation of this pedagogical element: we've
learned a great deal, but the learning is not over yet. We have to
be helped to catch on to values we haven't emphasized before,
take new and deeper views of life. Obedience lets the lifeblood
of the tradition flow in our veins, a tradition which has been
living these values successfully.

But part of this practice has another purpose: it is there to
open our eyes to what we are not, to what the human cannot be
until and unless it is filled with something beyond the human.
God and our participation in the divine life are not extras, not
ornaments, as it were, on the building of human life. They are
essential to the architecture of the person. In their obedience,
monks gather up a mature, independent personality and give it
to a transcendent Other in order to find its fulfillment, a fulfill-

ment which cannot be reached outside the redemption wrought by Christ.

What Do We Obey?

What do we obey?

Indeed, what? But first, whom? Well, a personal God, but one who has set up our lives as a share in his own. Obedience for anyone, lay or monastic, is a search for the mystery in which we are so essentially rooted that we cannot take our next breath in independence of its fostering presence, and yet for which we must always reach and long. Obedience is not so much a thing we do as a personal communion in the reverent surprise of being so personally and uniquely valued. We are seekers of divine celebration, no matter how heavy our feet along the way.

It is in obedience, formal or as manifested in the daily grind, that Christ lays his hand on the mechanism in us that compels us to achieve; the need to organize, analyze, determine. He does not destroy it: it has its place. But he touches it with reason and something more than reason — his own transcendent, redemptive life. Here the key is transcendence: our fulfillment. He has anointed us with his own spirit of passivity, of patience, with his own Passion.

Celibacy

We who live without a marital relationship, as well as those whose call has set them in any of the several states that grow out of marriage, meet in many places of the human heart, but chiefly in this: the fact that this heart is much too big for what's available to fill it.

Desire is made much of in monastic literature: this experience of not having what we really need, of not being what we really need to be, and of not being able to forget it. This desire can be a place in which we are almost a prisoner of our need to be filled, or at least of being not so *very* empty. And it can press hard, the not having a total human relationship, the kind of thing we imagine will fill that need.

But conversely, we see that no human relationship can answer that need. It is simply too great, and — on a human level — too unrealistic to be solved and pacified. We want too much. We want the perfect lover, mother, father, friend, the impossible other who will be so perfectly attuned to us that we will never need again.

People marry, and find out that this is not what they get. And when they have learned their way through this, they can begin to love the possible, and to pass through it to what we are all looking for. They begin to learn to love. If they are lucky.

We need the emptiness, and we get it whether we are married or not, and sometimes more painfully in marriage. We need the emptiness not only in order to relate to God, but in order to find the richness of human love, for this emptiness is the climate in which we can give ourselves to others and receive them back. It's by making peace with the emptiness, with a certain degree of frustration of our affective nature that we can make peace with the degree of support and the kind of love with which we are so liberally showered, the kind of love which is possible.

Prayer

The void we so often encounter in prayer is not an absence. It's an embrace; just as self-knowledge is not an experience of learning something unpleasant about ourselves, but one of those experiences created by the presence of the Christ who loves and needs us. For both things are the embrace of God, his moving in, his tenderness, his nearness. There is really no action of God toward us which is not a reaching out in desire for us, in desire for our happiness, our closeness to himself.

The starkness, the uncontrollability of prayer, the allowing ourselves to be held, is our permission to God to be himself toward us. It doesn't matter what we want it to become. We let go of it, of goals and expectations. We don't use it as an instrument in our tool box. We don't head into it with demands, but wait for him. And it can feel very much like Penelope, or like Margarete: being faithful to someone you married but who is becoming more and more unknown to you, who is growing beyond you, beyond your capacity for knowing him.

And only by entering this waiting stage, this want of understanding and satisfaction, can we find the peace of real prayer and come to want this lack of satisfaction more than any kind of excitement or emotional peace.

Sticking Your Neck Out

We began these reflections on the passive element of life by discarding all those synonyms which made it into a flabby sort of escape. But still it's a bit hard to understand how sticking one's neck out can involve so much of this passive aspect of spiritual growth.

There is a kind of meekness that avoids, in the name of virtue, not only constructive activity, but also constructive passivity. It should be obvious that a great deal of our lives demand of us a lot of plain, commonsense activity. Get this done; move that mountain; issue that protest; set this boundary; help your neighbor. Even, stop giving yourself to abuse. Stop this destructive relationship; you can't handle it. Now. It's no good running to hide under the eaves of a false idea of passivity. The will of God right now is get-out-and-do-it.

What's not always so clear is how certain types of receptive experience can invade our lives only when we are willing to stick our necks out. This applies to all of us — the big egos that go crashing into the china shop, and the naturally passive types, the fearful, shy people who burrow into the nearest little hill at the prospect of making a mess of something, at the approach of responsibility. And this includes the perfectionist who won't take on anything because it can't be done well enough, as well as that element in all of us which keeps an eye out for the man with the saw as we crawl out farther on our limb.

Keeping safe is not the name of true passivity. Avoiding re-

sponsibility, true mature thoughtfulness and initiative, is not a
receptive stance.

In taking on a task, we take on more than a love affair with
creative possibilities. We take on the compromises, limitations,
failures, stalls, retries, reorganization, and hurts of any enterprise, successful or unsuccessful. We take in hand at least one,
and probably a cat's cradle, of delicate and volatile human relationships. Through this rich texture runs the thread of the
given, the unbudging, the recalcitrant, and the impossible. In
some way, we will walk into the passive, in some way we will
meet the choice between accepting or revolting — the kind of
revolting that does not loosen the grip of the impossible.

Any realistic person who has taken on an executive position
knows that, however many its advantages, one of them is *not*
the opportunity to get other people automatically to do what
we want. Being in charge is a complicated business, and one of
its advantages is the opportunity to put oneself in the line of
fire. We are all too obviously visible and attackable; we become
the target for any number of criticisms, discontents, frustrated
ambitions, jealousies, and displaced resentments. Within this
emotional field we get our task accomplished or we can't. In
any case, we have agreed to come out of the hole in the hill
and experience true constructive passivity as an indispensable
component of active involvement and effective leadership.

Humiliation

Humiliation: who wants it? It can come in the sticking out of
one's neck or in the living of life in general, but uncomfortable
as it is, we might try to develop the courage to see it as a gift: an
invitation to acknowledge our own worth. For what forms the
pain of humiliation but an admission that we've been living by
comparison — as if comparison with someone else, with some
form of status or achievement, is the measure of our personal
worth, as if our position in someone's (or "everyone's") scale of
important people is what creates our value.

Our inner selves can be as tender as a running wound to the

touch of anything resembling rejection or inferiority. "Don't demean me or discard me or set me in a low rank. Don't leave me out. Let me be accomplished, accepted, triumphant. Make way for me."

And humiliation leaves us angry, nauseous, and afraid. But it's only saying in its turn, "You in yourself are worthy beyond expression. Recognition, accomplishment, a place on an upper rung do not constitute your value. They are ephemeral and unreliable guides to the place of your abiding worth. Consider the riches of your heart and the true beauty of your person. Rejoice that your value lies in something you never have to lose, in a stability which need never yield to the mathematics of comparison."

The Positive Passives

But what about the perfect (or even imperfect) pleasures of life? Have they no part in this passive element of growth? The shining September afternoons, warmth out of the cold, shade in the heat, music, art and dance, a child's litany of questions, a cat's silky grace — where do these fit? Right here. The receptive faculty can (and must) rest in the beautiful, in the refusal to submit every fraction of life to standards of function and utility.

A classical form of meditation does just this. It asks one sense at a time to receive a single element of the exterior world. We give over our sense of sight to a leaf, or a canopy of leaves through which the sun is shining, and really see this. Our whole self becomes a world of gentle attentiveness to these green shapes. Sight slows and calms us. It becomes a visual mantra.

Or taste. Or scent. Or the feel of things. It is regrettably possible to walk for ninety years on the brittle surface of a world that waits patiently to unfold its heart to us.

We can deliver ourselves to our sensual appetites in ways that violate ourselves and our world. Goering was an example of what happens when this rapacity goes crazy. He was, in Speer's opinion, the one man in Nazi leadership with the intelligence and popular following to moderate Hitler's policies or to stop the war at some point of rationality. But he was too radically imprisoned in material addictions to get up out of his wallow and exert his capabilities.

We can, however, consecrate our senses to the reception of God's self-revelation. This type of awareness — call it relaxation, meditation, mindfulness, presence, or whatever you like — is another form of giving oneself both gently and eagerly to the action of a world beyond ourselves, and to a world beyond all worlds. It too is a form of waiting, a bringing of our sensual appetites, which have at times betrayed us, into the place they were made for, into the healing, self-revealing bounty of God.

Part V

The Walker

Chapter 17

Emmaus

He walked with them in the cool of the evening (see Gen. 2).

That was in Paradise. God strolled about the garden while a light wind pushed away the day's heat and its labor. This is a restful image. The last hours of the day are given over to a special kind of companionship with God. He is not sitting under a tree as he did when calling on Abraham. He is present in movement, sharing his enjoyment of creation with the man and the woman. Together they watch the slanting sun of evening caught in the foliage of their garden. You can't imagine them loping or striding or rushing. The day is over, its goals have been met. They leave it gently where it is, and the appropriate verb for what they are doing now might be "wander."

Or perhaps in their minds they walk back through the day, slowly matching mental to material footsteps, ready to stop and touch and reverence; ready to consecrate in memory the vast daily simplicities they have so casually accepted.

Stay with Us, Lord

Now on that same day two of them were going to a village called Emmaus, about seven miles from Jerusalem, and talking with each other about all these things that had happened. While they were talking and discussing....
(Luke 24:13–15a NRSV)

This is also a Paradisal setting, but the story is much less simple. When Genesis uses the image, all is Paradise, and the only thing its people have to do is to be there, enjoy, admire, and belong to one another. Luke's story has more to do, and his use of the symbol expands its possibilities with great artistry.

To begin with, the two disciples are walking in the wrong direction. Unlike the primeval man and woman, they have a goal, one they shouldn't have. They are supposed to stay put. Jerusalem is where the story has been heading, and Jerusalem is where they should have stayed, waiting for a commission to leave. But they have checked out ahead of time, assuming there is nothing more to come, nothing more to wait for.

Secondly, they are trying to figure it out, stoking the little fires in each other's brains: blazes that feed on a search for reasons why nothing has worked right. They must have felt awful: everybody did. And they are trying to soothe their emotional pain with a search for explanation. We all do. The heart appeals to the head for meaning, and sometimes it gets what it asks for, and sometimes it doesn't. So the walk goes on, the talk goes on. And even though on a physical level, these men have a goal — the wrong one — they are walking around in circles on the level of the mind.

Then Jesus himself draws near and goes with them.

Two things are happening. Jesus "draws near," a beautifully significant verb, and "goes with" them. The Gospels brim with, "he went." During his ministerial years, the verb emphasizes his human limitations and opportunities: he could not simply be in one place, then in another. There was a space between and he had to cover it. He walked, mostly, and in consequence, he felt, smelled, heard, and saw what the road had to offer.

The risen Jesus tends instead to drop in out of nowhere. And maybe he did so now. Maybe they only assumed he had come up from behind and overtaken them. But at any rate, we find again, "he went." He measures his Easter steps to theirs and walks from where they should have been to where they were going. He draws "near" and walks "with" them. And here Luke begins to weave another major symbol into his story. Their eyes were "held" from recognizing him.

It is at least possible that Genesis means to convey an image of the primeval man and his wife "seeing" the God who took his leisure with them in their garden, knowing quite well who he was. Never mind that God is pure spirit: in this kind of story they may have been able to see him, for in it he has hands and breath and voice. Seeing went with walking and did not need to be mentioned. The scene was uncluttered.

But the Emmaus story is cluttered exceedingly. Luke, as I mentioned, has a far more complex scene on his hands, for he is dealing, not with creation, but with re-creation; not with primeval innocence, but with the distorted and destructive human situation struggling with (or against) its salvation.

They did not see. Their eyes were held. Eyes that had been made for seeing were being held. By what? By their own expectations? "We had hoped," they say. "We had our own plans for him, we had our own plans for ourselves." And one's own plans can narrow the field of vision, as we have seen with Speer.

Or perhaps they were blinded by a poor formation in the spiritual life. Or by their own psychological limitations. Then, after all, no one could have been prepared to encounter on a country road a man who had just died and been buried. They brought with them in addition only the further confusion of those wild, necessarily grief-ridden stories of the women. Some of their group had gone, and yes, the tomb was empty, "but him they did not see." Those who had approached the empty tomb were no better at seeing than our friends on the road.

Jesus does not treat them as Paul was to be treated — Paul, with his own case of obstructed vision. Jesus will not discuss matters with Paul, and we can understand why. Even God would not relish an argument with Paul. Paul he shut up without a chance to get a word in. With Cleophas and his companion, however, the Lord converses. He asks and listens before he gives his own account. "Was it not fitting...?" Was it not right, was it not the only way? Should not the Christ have wrestled death to the ground by dying himself in terrible pain?

They were to remember afterward that their hearts were burning as he spoke — not, this time, their heads. Their overworked heads have been drawn down into some previously unexplored region of the heart, and more than light is given. Fire also.

They asked him to stay on. This is important; time is important. Evening is coming on and the day is now far spent. We remember other walks and conversations in the evening breeze of a garden. We feel now the weariness of a race grown old, very far away from that primeval garden, trudging the wrong roads in the wrong direction. Stay with us, sir. Stay with us, Lord. The day is almost over. Stay.

And then they see. They recognize that their dusty fellow pilgrim is more than they have thought him. And in the moment of recognition, he vanishes. Their eyes lose him whom their hearts have come to know.

The text does not say he left, but only that he vanished from their sight. In this moment of conversion, they turn around and, walking still, take the road back to Jerusalem, to the place of another encounter and of a sending forth. Their footsteps now and ever are conversion.

But notice. While they were walking in the wrong direction, they could not recognize him, visible as he was. When they had turned and walked in the right direction, they still could not see him, for he had vanished.

Drawing near, he had gone with them. He never ceased to; they simply could not see him who had never left. But the failure to see which followed their conversion was not at all the same as that which had preceded it. He trusted them with one moment of sight but a lifetime of presence, one moment of recognition and a lifetime of learning to see in a different way. He placed in their hearts a lifetime of faith.

More Than "They"

We've been saying, "they," and thinking of two specific men on a specific road on a specific day in the history of the world. But Luke means more than that when he says "they" and "road" and "day." He means us. He means now. And he means Albert Speer.

Early Christians were known as people of the Way, walkers of the road, for their belief was called just that: the Way, the road. And "that very day," Easter Day, is *today*, now. I remember reading Peter's sermon from Acts at the Easter Sunday Eucharist: "Now we are those witnesses — we have eaten and drunk with him after his resurrection from the dead," and thinking, "Oh, wow, that's us. That's right now, this Eucharist, this moment." It is always "that very day," always Easter Day, and Christ is always drawing near, always walking beside us. It is always his road, whether we recognize him, or like Speer, mostly do not.

For the prayer-life of Albert Speer was an Emmaus journey, the story of a road, an inner and an outer road, and a different kind of presence.

Chapter 18

The Road

Their eyes were held. (I like that expression. It evokes a hand gently pressed to the eyes, a shielding hand.) There can be many reasons why Jesus chooses to hide his visible presence from us.

In Speer's case, we can easily account for much of the emotional and doctrinal austerity of his relationship with God. Adolf Hitler was not much of a spiritual director, although Speer was sharp enough to see in Hitler a deformed religious sensibility. Speer's own upbringing had not given him a doctrinal or practical basis for mature faith. Twice he mentions that in the dining room of his parents' home, family festivals were still celebrated, as his baptismal party had been. It seems a casual remark, but by the time of writing, he had read enough theology to realize the importance of Christian baptism. In him, the sacrament had lain neglected for forty years. But at Spandau, whether he knew it or not, whether his eyes were held or open, the fact of his baptism worked its way through day after oppressive day and wrought its redemptive mission in his life and prayer.

Eric Sevareid emerged from World War II and great personal tragedy with a deep longing for belief, for relationship with a God to whom he could bring his acquaintance with human depravity and suffering, a faith that would give him meaning. But he says he could neither find his way back to his religious roots, nor discover a faith more capable of integrating his mature experience. So he left that longing where it lay, and moved on.[72] Speer had no place to move on to, and so he faced what Sevareid had faced — the moral wasteland of World War II — as well as a burden of personal guilt whose dimensions the human spirit has rarely been asked to accept. And through that wilderness he walked with God, though not exactly a God of consolation.

What Is to Hand

When you don't have much, you use what you have. Speer began by using what was to hand: the absurdly simple, conventional means available to anyone. He went to church on Sunday.

Of the Nuremberg months, he was to write:

The Sunday divine services became a great support for me. Even as recently as my stay in Kransberg I had refused to attend them. I did not want to seem soft. But in Nuremberg I threw aside such prideful feelings. The pressure of circumstances brought me — as, incidentally, it did almost all the defendants with the exception of Hess, Rosenberg, and Streicher — into our small chapel.[73]

Before their removal to Spandau, the convicted defendants attended Good Friday services in a balcony of the local church, segregated from the congregation.

In Spandau:

Today, Saturday, we had our first Spandau religious service, in a double cell converted into a chapel. Bare walls painted light brown, a prison table for altar, a Bible on it, a simple wooden cross on the wall behind. Six prison chairs, for Hess will still not take part in the services. In the corner the cell toilet, with a wooden cover. A Soviet supervising officer sat down on it.[74]

He could distinguish between faith and the feeling of faith and recognize how easily circumstance can erode a sense of believing ("He vanished from their sight"). Yet Speer remained faithful to his vanished companion, *doing* his belief when often his inner eyes had no more than feeble sight.

Jan. 1, 1947. Began the new year dispiritedly. Swept corridor, a walk, and then to church. Doenitz and I sing more loudly than usual because Raeder is sick and Funk is due to go to the hospital. Only the pressure I was under during the trial made me believe that I believed. Since then I again have the feeling of meaningless rituals during the church services. The narrowness of man's perspective. But these are only the most obvious conditions that color our thoughts. How many conditions must every proposition be subject to, conditions we do not even suspect?[75]

Dec. 24, 1954. I was rolled to the chapel on a stretcher. But I had to stay lying down during the service.[76]

March 21, 1959. Now we have a one-man parish in Spandau. For weeks Schirach has sent his excuses to the chaplain, though he gives no reason for his absence. And so I sit opposite the chaplain alone. It is equally embarrassing to us both that he, standing two paces away, preaches down at me. He was therefore relieved when I proposed today that he deliver his sermon sitting. Not that this helps very much. In this situation the solemnity of divine worship simply will not come.[77]

He went to church. That could be counted as little enough or great indeed, depending on your viewpoint. But what was he taking to that wretched chapel with a toilet in the corner? Auschwitz, Ravensbruk, Etty Hillsom, the London Blitz, Omaha Beach? He didn't have a wasted life to bring. "Wasted" is an anemic adjective to describe a life like his. And yet what other word to use? The dramatic words have an overwrought character. They dramatize what is really not dramatic. Most simply said, he brought conversion. He brought that moment to which a long walk in the wrong direction had been leading, and the slow, dogged trek along the road back.

Church-going was not all there was to it. He read philosophy and theology, struggling with Barth's *Dogmatik*. Someone told Barth, who was very pleased.

I have by now read six volumes of Barth's Dogmatik.
*There is much that I still cannot comprehend, chiefly be-
cause of the difficulty of the terminology and the subject.
But I have had a curious experience. The uncomprehended
passages exert a tranquilizing effect. With Barth's help I
feel in balance and actually, in spite of all that's oppressive,
as if liberated.*[78]

This is somber theology. "Man is by nature evil" unhinges
the sensibilities I have developed from my own tradition, and
I wished him some of St. Bernard — Bernard, of whom Luther
had been an admirer. For Bernard has a way of displaying the
length and breadth of moral evil in a set of verbal fireworks,
then letting the fire burn steadily into an exposition of human
dignity and the glory of our intimacy with a redeeming God.
The nature whose faculties have been twisted and darkened
retains the image of God, capable of embracing a vast and
glorious redemption.

However, Speer was given one thing that his situation made
easy to assimilate — a sense of the value of his punishment, a
value which in some mysterious way was calling back those
forty years from the hell they had created and in which they
had buried themselves.

*I owe to Barth the insight that man's responsibility is not
relieved just because evil is part of his nature. Man is by
nature evil and nevertheless responsible. It seems to me
there is a kind of complement to that idea in Plato's state-
ment that for a man who has committed a wrong "there is
only one salvation: punishment." Plato continues: "Therefore it is better for him to suffer this punishment than to
escape it; for it sustains man's inward being."*[79]

He kept on walking, choosing, doing — and, in his own way,
seeing. No, church-going was not enough.

The French chaplain, Casalis, gave a sermon on the subject:

*"The lepers in Israel were cut off from the community
of the people by a host of legal prohibitions; these were*

as insurmountable as a prison wall." Raeder, Doenitz, and Schirach take offense; they contend that the chaplain called them "lepers." Fierce discussions rage in the yard and the washroom. I keep out of them.

The situation is probably this: they don't want to hear any truths from the chaplain. In spite of all that has happened, to them the Church is merely a part of the scenery of respectability. No more. It's there for baptisms, weddings, deaths, but it isn't supposed to meddle with questions of conscience. One more instance of how little this class of bourgeois leaders appreciates the moral implications of Christian doctrine. No opposition to the atrocities could be expected on that basis, certainly. Thoughts about the connection between Christian decadence and barbarization. When at the end of the war I decided on active opposition, my stand was not that of a Christian, but of a technocrat. Then how am I different from my fellow prisoners? In the final analysis probably only because I see such connections and can accept Casalis' sermon as a challenge.[80]

We find many passages like this, in which an initial judgment of others, harsh but truthful, is later either softened or turned in upon himself. And yet the self-criticism is realistic: he does not brutalize himself. He judges himself as a practical man bearing a burden of incalculable weight, yet willing to do what is possible in carrying it a little farther down the road.

Before the service Raeder officially protested to Chaplain Casalis, in the name of five of his fellow prisoners, because the chaplain had referred to them as lepers. They were asking him to preach the Gospel and nothing else. I deliberately took the opposite view, saying, "I am not a neurasthenic. I would rather not be treated delicately. Your sermons should upset me." Much ill feeling.[81]

The ill feeling is understandable; it must have come across as unbearably self-righteous. But the difference of outlook in such an emotional situation was too raw to admit of rational accommodation.

A View from the Top

Speer was not a mountain climber, in the sense of someone who grapples with sheer faces of rock and snow-laden summits. He did, however, in his youth, walk much in the mountains, and tells of stubbornly pushing on through terrible weather, even though when he got to the ridge which would normally have a view, the vista was as fogged out as he had known it would be. We can feel something of this in one of his most revealing statements on the spiritual life.

> *A few weeks ago, Casalis gave me Karl Barth's* Epistle to the Romans. *Barth phrases everything with great firmness. That appeals to me. As I understand him, the Christian commandments represent virtually infinite values, which even a saint can only approximate. It is given to no one to remain without fault. Every human being inevitably sins. But I must confess that for pages at a time I could scarcely grasp Barth's thought. After the services today I said to Casalis that faith seems to me like a tremendous mountain range. Tempting from a distance, when you try to climb it you run into ravines, perpendicular walls, and stretches of glacier. Most climbers are forced to turn back; some plunge to destruction; but almost nobody reaches the peak. Yet the world from on top must offer a wonderfully novel and clear view.*[82]

It is this disjunction between what he felt he could do and what he felt the life of the spirit demanded that makes me uneasy. It may be a sad element in his spiritual understanding. We have to feel that what we're asked to do is possible, and I'm not sure he ever did. His fidelity to the journey is remarkable, given this deprivation. Chaplain Casalis surely helped him, but perhaps the effect of his own spiritual outlook on Speer's personality was not altogether constructive.

Physically, Spandau offered its inmates only level ground to walk on, no hills. But of this he took full advantage. Walking, like his garden, was to become an unrecognized symbol of what God was achieving in him. The qualities of his walk came to reflect the characteristics of his prayer.

This is interesting, isn't it? We tend to think of prayer as stillness. Our instinctive image for prayer would not be Emmaus but Mary of Bethany. And yet prayer, though rightly imaged as stillness, can also be recognized as movement.

The Walk

We have seen that regular exercise was, from the first, an element in Speer's program of prison survival. The garden had its place in this scheme; so did walking. He constructed an elliptical path around the garden and counted its length with his feet. Then so many laps would equal so many kilometers. Hess gave him the idea of counting laps by shifting beans from one pocket to another.

> *I have a new idea to make myself exercise to the point of exhaustion: I have begun, along with the garden work, to walk the distance from Berlin to Heidelberg — 626 kilometers! For that purpose I have marked out a circular course in the garden.... If I had taken a different route, along the prison wall, I could have made my track 350 meters. But because of the better view, I prefer this other track. This project is a training of the will, a battle against the endless boredom; but it is also an expression of the last remnants of my urge toward status and activity.*[83]

Funk watched, frowning. "I suppose you want to become a suburban letter-carrier?"[84]

But even this grew unsatisfactory.

> *By sheer chance, on this day I completed the last stage on the walk to Heidelberg. While I was still tramping my rounds in the garden, Hess came out and sat down*

on his bench.... "Now I am setting out for Munich," I said as I passed him on the next-to-last round. "Then on to Rome and down as far as Sicily. Sicily's in the Mediterranean, so I won't be able to walk any farther." "... Why not by way of the Balkans to Asia?" Hess asked. "Everything there is Communist," I replied. "But maybe I could go by way of Yugoslavia to Greece. And from there through Salonika, Constantinople, and Ankara to Persia." Hess nodded. "That way you could reach China." I shook my head. "Communist too.... The more interesting route would be through Aleppo, Beirut, Baghdad, and across the desert to Persepolis and Teheran. A long, hot tramp, lots of desert. I hope I'll find oases. At any rate, I have a good program now.... You've helped me out of an embarrassing predicament. Many, many thanks, Herr Hess." With the hint of a bow, as though we were at a diplomatic reception, Hess replied, "Most pleased to be of help, Herr Speer."[85]

On the stretch from Salzburg to Vienna, I several times had to fight boredom; several times I was on the point of quitting the whole thing. Merely covering distance no longer satisfies me; it's too abstract just to count the kilometers. I must make it all more vivid. Perhaps I should take the idea of hiking around the world quite literally and conceive each segment in full detail. For that purpose I would have to obtain maps and books and familiarize myself fully with the segment immediately ahead: the landscape, the climate, the people and their culture, their occupations, their manner of life.[86]

By the time he was released from Spandau, he had "walked around the world." As Spandau's garden expressed something of his conversion experience, so also did this remarkable accomplishment. It was not a deliberate form of prayer, but like many other enterprises in life, it turned out to have a meaning of its own. In this case, like a drama, it unfolded another aspect of his inward journey.

Enclosure

For one thing, he walked within an enclosure. There were material walls around Spandau, and emotional walls around Speer's heart: his guilt, his personal reticence, his loneliness, and the limitations of his religious background. God for him was not a pleasant companion, and his journey was neither a diversion nor an adventure.

Yet he walked enormous distances in the world of the spirit — not only in spite of these limiting factors but because of them. Because of their effects on his inner world, he had access to desert places and treeless plains. He could walk with a God stripped of illusory comfort and compensation, a Christ who seemed to vanish into these restricting psychological elements and to withdraw everything in the image of himself that was less real than himself.

Around the World

Secondly, he walked around the world, the world of geographical and cultural differences, the world of human striving, sorrow, and growth. He had not been, since his own moment at Emmaus, concerned only for himself. He cared about the world, about the other, whether this "other" were the people of Germany, its prisoners of war, his family, or what we have learned to call the family of nations. The original motivating force of his conversion had been the intention to save Germany; this broadened into the desire that his own condemnation at Nuremberg should affect the future conduct of all nations. He returns more than once to these defeated hopes:

> *The papers in recent days have carried brief accounts on the back pages to the effect that the UN is still debating whether the Nuremberg principles are to be acknowledged as a basis for international law. Naturally Doenitz, Schirach, and Raeder have been making taunting remarks, as though this constituted a personal defeat for me. And in*

*fact I admit that my view of myself is affected by it. For to
me Nuremberg was never just a settling of accounts with
past crimes. Rather, to this day I have drawn strength from
the hope that the trial's principles would become international law. Now it turns out that evidently only a few
nations are willing to accept it. What can I do in the face
of recriminations but remain silent?*[87]

He did not realize that something was happening on the
impalpable level of grace, or that Christ not only walked beside him but within him, identifying Speer's prison road with
his own Way of the Cross. The prisoner's eyes were held,
and so this he did not see, did not see his own redemptive mission in the history of the world, and the grace which
flowed from it, far surpassing his limited — and often disappointed — hopes. "What can I do...but remain silent?" falls
like a twentieth-century echo of the Passion account.

His own conception of his prayer was humble and commonplace. Elijah, feeling his life was over, had prayed for death.
Speer felt that way too, and only a sense of responsibility toward his family and toward the world for which his book
would be a warning and a confession gave him the power
to survive depression and the prison's devaluation of his personal worth. What could he do for the people he loved, these
others outside himself and his pain? He could hide from them
his anguish (the questionable choice of a reticent temperament
afraid of breaking down before them and thus increasing their
suffering), and he could pray for them.

*Before going to sleep read the Apostle Paul's Epistle to the
Romans. In spite of all the spiritual aid, I have been living
for many years in a kind of spiritual isolation. Sometimes
I think about death. But it is rather because I have had
enough of life. Only the thought of the children....And
then the book! That is gradually displacing architecture. It
is becoming the sole task I can still see ahead. Otherwise,
I expect nothing more.*[88]

*March 19, 1955. My fiftieth birthday. . . . Went to bed early
and will, as I often do, pray for the happiness of family
and friends.*[89]

He also developed a custom of praying for any unknown persons who had heard of him and prayed for him. I have found it very moving to know that in this way he prayed for me, and for those whom his books have introduced to his life.

Anticipation of returning to his family was not an unmixed blessing. What would they do with a sixty-year-old stranger? In the event, his fears were to prove well founded. And yet he kept on walking toward them. Elijah walked forty days and forty nights to the mountain of God in the strength of the food given him. And Speer walked twenty years on the strength of the food of his love for others.

The Whisper of a Breeze

To Elijah, God came in the whisper of a breeze; to Speer also, as a presence almost too fragile and impalpable to acknowledge. And yet he did acknowledge it, in his own reserved and primitive and monumental testimony:

*January 28, 1962. I am writing this as a profession of
faith: I believe in a divine providence; I also believe in
God's wisdom and goodness; I trust in his ways, even
though they may seem matters of chance. It is not the
mighty of the earth who determine the course of history.
They think they are the movers, and they are moved.*[90]

The Circle

Thirdly, he walked in a circle—not a small one, but around and around the garden; day after day, lap after lap, over and over the same ground. It's a paradox: limitation and expansion. But also it's the paradox of going around in circles in order to get somewhere, and of having to find and refind your starting place.

It's a matter of coming back to the beginning over and over, of putting your feet in your own footprints over and over, of learning the road till you can walk it with your eyes closed, and then falling over a stone you've passed a thousand times. Or getting a thrill of discovery out of a time of day whose feel you thought you had memorized.

It's coming back, starting again, learning what you thought you knew, unlearning what you were so attached to that you couldn't see that it was blinding you to what was there. This return is interesting, for it occurs on many levels. Speer examined and reexamined the past which had brought him to Spandau, and so grew in understanding of the world and the individual man — Albert Speer — that this past disclosed. But the past was only the starting point, the recurring beginning from which he went on to newer and richer spiritual places.

And he seemed to be walking alone. It's no fun to walk with a God you cannot feel. You would really like to feel him. It would be a kind of seeing.

Remember the disciples of Emmaus, discussing. That's what they were doing: discussing why Jesus wasn't there, when he was. There's a lot of discussing in Speer's diaries too. That's the human thing. We try to understand, to get oriented, to grasp this invisible lover — with our minds if he is so successful at escaping our emotions. We itch and scratch, unless we atrophy altogether.

Sometimes, the physical act of walking can itself pacify our desperation. And as a symbol it can be an acted prayer, a way of acquiescing in the decision of Christ to walk unseen beside us.

The Unfelt Love

God often gives us, too, the simplicity of an unfelt love, an unfelt presence. It's impossible for our experience to equal Speer's for austerity, for sheer apophatic doggedness. He was deprived of something we take for granted, and sometimes even resent: the blessing of doctrine. Yet even for us, it's not easy to live with an invisible God, a God with whom we're going around in circles.

Iris

The path in Spandau's garden was edged with iris. Iris is the rainbow flower, for Iris was the goddess of the rainbow, and it is always symbolic, as the bow in Genesis: never again would the waters of the flood invade the earth.

A rainbow is not flamboyant. It doesn't shout. It's understated, like the quiet presence of God to the journey of the contemplative. The vision of it comes and goes like Jesus at Emmaus. It can't be laid hold of and packed away and stored and opened on demand.

It attends the storm.

And in Speer's case, I think a conscience like his, colored by the blood of Buchenwald and London, and by the blood of Christ himself, stood like a kind of rainbow above the receding floodwaters of Hitler's Europe. The life of Albert Speer is eminently baptismal, a life immersed in a different kind of flood — the redemptive death of Christ — and sharing the quiet glory of an Easter morning. The beds of iris he passed so many times a day imaged this baptismal triumph he so dimly understood.

The Triumph

It was a different sort of triumph, wasn't it, from the kind of thing he had planned to immortalize in hyperbolic stone? The man who had designed palaces and arches for a demented murderer had immersed himself in the glory of everyday common services.

So many things can express a life of prayer: and so it was for him — the laundry, the reverent use of his senses, the bearing of others' burdens, and the pride he took in renovating the chapel which had held his faithful worship for so long. He considered himself a monk, and after his release, experienced a sense of

alienation from the world to which he had returned. Spandau
had been the home of his solitude and of his discovery of God.

After the death of Rudolf Hess, the Allied Powers had Spandau Prison razed, uneasy at the prospect of its becoming a Nazi
shrine. They had a shopping mall built on the site. When I
learned this, my heart ached. I had felt, like Jacob, that this
was holy ground.

Part VI

The Others

Chapter 19

The Others

I have taken a dark view of Speer's fellow prisoners. Yet often his descriptions of them can pull urgently at one's heart: his compassionate portrait of Hess, his respect for Neurath, his portrait of the pathetic self-destruction of Funk. But for good or ill, and for all his inner and outer solitude, the conversion of Albert Speer proceeded in company.

How many of us would say that the principal factor in the journey of conversion is the people we live with? Yes, prayer is essential, and liturgy. Certainly grace. And obviously the big things of which these others are expressions: the Incarnation, the paschal sacrifice.

But on a practical daily level, what tips us into the grace? What constitutes a great deal of the substance of prayer, overturns our expectations, defenses, illusions, refusals to move? What draws out our confidence or diminishes it, melts our defenses or reinforces them? What shows us what's inside us?

Isn't it the husband or wife, the children, the people at work, someone whose natural or supernatural superiority agitates our sense of worthlessness, the persevering kindness of someone who believes in us, the sense of belonging or of not belonging, the thousand demands for skills of mature relationship, the way in which working with — or without — others affects us?

So why do I talk about it last? Because, though it is a part of the basic adventure of conversion, it is also, and eminently, an outgrowth of it. It is not just one more thing to do, as if Christian obligations were all lined up side by side on a shelf and nicely separate and labeled. It is an organic outgrowth of all we've been talking about until now.

This is easy to see: what we tried to do early on in our life of grace becomes possible (and sometimes even easy, as St. Benedict says) not because we have kept at it — though we've tried to — but because we've gone through the conversion mill: self-knowledge, helplessness, forgiveness. Our relationships and sense of community have been kneaded into grace and prayer, into a sense of moral and spiritual destitution and the intimate experience of personal salvation.

Speer's Community

The inmates of Spandau were an uncongenial lot. At one point, Speer had been given a week of solitary for some minor infraction of rules and writes of his fellow inmates:

> *I am avoided by Funk, Schirach, and Raeder. They have predicted to the guards that my collapse will come today. Evidently my calmness irritates them. Strange, what has happened to us. What animosities thrive under conditions of excessive proximity!*[91]

Speer's moral stance alienated his fellow prisoners. After all, if he held himself guilty for the brutalities of the war, he was implicitly inviting them to the same accountability, one they did not want to accept. In addition, prison conditions played on their emotional weaknesses and questioned their moral values. Most practically, at the best of times these men all lacked relational skills.

But they had humor; and I have laughed aloud — and still do — at passages in the diaries.

> *Frederick [a guard] is bringing in Hennessy and Canadian Club. Temporary change of mood. The children will wonder about my exuberant official letter. Doenitz has written his Sunday letter in verse. This jollity should make an attentive censor suspicious.*[92]

> *Funk sneaks around in the corridor. A French guard is snoring. Far away I hear someone unlocking a door. To*

*Funk: "Quick, wake Monsieur Corgnol up." It is only
common decency to alert a sleeping guard when someone is coming. What else is there for them to do but
sleep? False alarm. Corgnol unlocks my door. "Would you
like to stroll in the corridor? If someone comes go right
back in."*[93]

*This month the meat smells and tastes abominable.
Schirach commented in disgust, "When I find a cat's
whiskers in the goulash, the secret will be out."*[94]

The Unsupported Ego

When Speer was armaments minister and Doenitz Commander
of the German Navy, they were friends.

*Stimulated by yesterday's argument, I have been trying
to call the other Doenitz to mind....He was always de-
cent and reliable, and made an excellent impression on
me. Despite the clouding of our relationship in the course
of our imprisonment, I remember our collaboration with
pleasure.*[95]

When both egos were unsupported, when Speer was no
longer a minister of the cabinet and Doenitz a highly respected admiral, " ... my relations with Doenitz have continued
to deteriorate."

*I understand why he has held aloof from me, and respect
his reasons. Moreover, he has been gripped by the psy-
chosis of a prisoner who dashes his head against the wall
of his verdict and sentence. Such refusal to accept often
produces unexpected, uncontrollable reactions.*[96]

Doenitz was particularly sensitive to Speer's acknowledgment of guilt, for Doenitz maintained his innocence — and his
importance — until his dying day.

*He complained bitterly that everybody still speaks of
Rommel as the "field marshal" while he and Raeder are*

always merely called "the former grand admirals." "The
thing is ridiculous," he said. "Even under international
law the rank of grand admiral is just as irrevocable as that
of field marshal." I forbore to remind him that he had not
come forth with this opinion when after July 20 his fellow
officers had their rank revoked, and were in fact expelled
from the army, so that Hitler could hang them.[97]

He and Speer were never reconciled. They viewed basic values far too differently. On the last day they saw one another, the
day of Doenitz's release, Speer's control broke, and their conflict burst into anger. The miracle was that they had not been
shouting at each other for ten years.

The Nature of Spandau's Community

The most interesting theme in the diaries, next to Speer's conversion, is the study of the complete noncommunity of its
community, its pettiness:

Funk has created a kind of arbor by planting many sun-
flowers in a square. Today the order came to remove these
sunflowers because they interfered with observation. The
order produced something like a nervous breakdown in
most of us. Funk, outraged, formally resigned his office as
chief gardener. Schirach lopped off his flowers, which were
in no way being threatened, and Doenitz destroyed his
beds of beans. Rostlam watched us, stunned. He seemed
really troubled. "Like children! In our prisons you'd get
one week of solitary confinement on bread and water."
The incident shows how fragile our equanimity is, and
how thin-skinned we have become.[98]

Ill-humor for days. Without asking our admiralty, I re-
cently did my laundry a day earlier than usual. Even today,
four days afterward, Doenitz and Raeder stood together
discussing my behavior. "Another of his explosive deci-

sions! An idea leaps into his head and he's got to carry it out right off. He doesn't ever pause to consider."[99]

What could hardly be called even an approach to community rapidly gave way to the effects of a restricted, demeaning environment. Status — lost and imaginary or incredibly petty — obsessed the personalities of men robbed of the self-importance for which they had lived.

[Doenitz:] *"But I am still and will remain the legal chief of state. Until I die!"*[100]

One person used another, not out of friendship, but for some kind of compensation or to satisfy a desperate need for company. One of the most pathetic manifestations of human deterioration was the leaving out of the difficult personality.

I have conducted a kind of opinion poll to measure our prestige among the guards. The special aspect of it is that none of those involved knows anything about it — neither those whose popularity is to be measured, not those who are being polled. My procedure is this: the order in which we fetch our meals is decided by the guards. They are aware that each of us, oddly enough, would like to be first. The degree of their liking decides whom they will let out of the cell first. I give the first man three points, the second two, the third one, and the last none. After a week, Funk leads with forty-nine points, and Schirach is just ahead of me with thirty-nine points. I have thirty-six points, whereas Hess is credited with only two — only once was he let out second, otherwise always last. For the first time I realize that this troublesome, sick man has been getting his meals last for ten years.[101]

What Was Wrong

The whole prison story forms a wonderful case study in how not to live community — monastic, family, or otherwise. But we also learn from it why we have trouble with one another. And it shows all too graphically why the conversion we've been talking about has to open onto community, and how community grows out of the conversion process.

Remember the lust for achievement, for success and status? This, denied, unconfronted, and unworked-through, soured the relationships in Spandau.

Remember the necessity for self-knowledge? All sorts of conflict, bitter and unresolved, erupted among these men who did not know why they were acting as they were.

Remember the need to accept phases and experiences of helplessness, passivity, restriction, and negation, to see these things in a positive light? The restrictive environment of Spandau rubbed raw the conventions by which these men had lived. They could not bear the loss of ego support and took it out on each other.

Remember the acceptance of a silent God, a God who has some relation to one's moral dilemma? To these men, God was a convention rather than a challenge or companion, much less the one who loves and is desired for himself. So he had no effect on community, or on the mental and spiritual growth which could have developed community.

The Guards

I have said that Speer never really confronted the possibility of believing himself forgiven and that his only manner of accepting forgiveness had to be, not only implicit, but also mediated and concrete. He accepted the forgiveness of God in accepting the forgiveness of other men. As early as Nuremberg, he would say:

> *Every day I learn how inhuman we really were. Now I do not mean the barbarism of persecution and extermination. Rather, the absolute dominion of utilitarian ends, such as I pursued as minister of armaments, is nothing but a form of inhumanity. The American soldiers who guard us are coal miners, oil drillers, farm laborers. Detached from divisions that took an active part in the fighting,*

*many of them wear military decorations whose meaning
is unknown to me. The rules call for rigorous standards
of guarding, but these men always balance the rigor by
kindness. There is never any sign of sadism. John, a miner
from Pennsylvania, has actually become something close
to a friend. It is striking that the Negro American soldiers
were the first to overcome the barrier of hostility. Partly on
the basis of their own experiences, they seemed to regard
us as underdogs who deserve pity. Even more impressive
was the behavior of several Jewish doctors. Even Streicher,
who was despised and treated insultingly by almost everyone, including us, his fellow defendants, received support
from them far beyond the measure imposed by their duty
as physicians.*[102]

This relationship with the guards at Spandau had its negative
aspects.

*Sharkov, who hitherto has always been friendly and help-
ful, has for the past several weeks been surly and even
hostile. I have no idea what the reason is.... Not only the
prisoners, the guards too are being deformed. What de-
forms them is the right to exhibit any kind of ill-humor.*[103]

But on the whole, their presence to Speer and the other
prisoners was remarkably positive.

*Yesterday half an hour with Ulf, today with Hilde. Such
visits after a gap of a year remain strangely unreal and
at the same time painful. By strict control, I try to keep
down any expression of emotion, for that would make me
lose my composure entirely. Afterwards, when the children
have gone, I feel exhilarated every time, however badly the
conversations went. I pour out on the guards a veritable
torrent of words.*[104]

*Solin, the nice new Russian, today picked a few raspber-
ries still left on the everbearing canes here and there, and
brought them to me on a rhubarb leaf.*[105]

A few days ago, Colonel Bird casually asked me about the customary Christmas dinner in our family. This evening, in accordance with my reply, there was boiled ham, potato salad, horseradish, and asparagus. For dessert, as at home, chocolate ice cream. The asparagus was a mistake, but one I may introduce to the family. The colonel was present when the food was served. As I heard later that evening, he bought all these special things himself and paid for them out of his own pocket.[106]

Solitude

There is a type of solitude which only other people can create. We can reject this difficult kind of solitude in the name of solitude, or in the name of community — even though it is necessary for conversion and, consequently, for the development of true community.

What are its contributing elements? We've talked about some, but there are others. Being disagreed with is one: not having oneself affirmed by having other people share the opinions with which we have identified emotionally.

Or loneliness, the kind you feel when surrounded by people whom you know by experience can go only so far in alleviating the void within. Then let my solitude embrace the people who are causing it. This is their service to me.

How about changes, or want of changes? Experiences of dispensability — even someone else's — can create a particularly piercing kind of solitude. I remember a meeting in which one of those present brought the greeting of someone who had been highly regarded by the group — the kind of builder and molder of action without whom no one could imagine proceeding. He was retired now, and things were going on well without him. Another greeting from another fallen pillar; and everyone laughed. I thought to myself that it really wasn't funny; no one's dispensability is. The importance of everyone present was just that flimsy, and the sense was not so much of vulnerability as of mortality.

Naturally, there is also a kindness, an interest in the other, that makes, together with solitude, a kind of fabric in which the conversion takes place. But our shelves are lined with books about that. We hear less often or we think less often, about the usefulness of what's wrong — what's wrong with communities and what's wrong with the people who contribute to the common disasters.

Community and What's Wrong

What's wrong with community can be as helpful as what's right. And so often, what's wrong is not really what's wrong. What's wrong is its effect on my sense of self-worth. It's not the faults of others that get me down — or their virtues, which can be equally annoying. It's what their faults or their virtues are doing to deprive me of the self I want to be. Or how they are at least rescraping the raw skin of a damaged self-image. Someone else is not reflecting back to me the self I am projecting. Or someone is treading roughly on the ruins of the job that has already been done to my projected self. My problem with people can be that they do not concede my worth on the terms in which I am demanding it. Or someone else's problem may be encountering mine, and the two weak egos blow each other up. Or I let someone else's problem get inside me and determine my own emotional weather.

The Reason for What Is Wrong

What's wrong is someone's ministry to me. God has permitted some people to bear the burden of weakness, of incompleteness, of not seeing themselves accurately. And he has permitted this for my sake. Not to "try" me, but to draw me to himself. This bitter ministry corresponds to my need. Let someone else's disability do its healing work in me. If I'm addicted to affirmation, if I'm a compulsive judge and analyzer of other people's actions and motives, if I can't be disagreed with, if I have to have the

co-workers I want, the family I want, made to my own specifications, if my spiritual life "needs" this and this and this and
cannot survive only on God's allowance of it, then I have to let
go of what I have to have, of what I am demanding others to
be. And they will help me to loosen my grip if I can see the
benefit of this.

They will not be cut to my specifications. And I can't be
helped by them if my vision of them is blocked by what I am demanding them to be, if my agenda is to reform them according
to the pattern of my emotional "needs."

Reverence

People who are deprived emotionally are sacred people, sacred places. I may have tried to help them and failed. I may
want to make them over and can't. But I can always respect
them because they are entrusted with a particularly deep share
in Christ's redemptive care for us. Very often, the delay in
their development is their paschal offering; it can hurt them a
lot, and it is meant to fill our need. Probably the erratic behavior that gets me down is their way of coping with things
they aren't yet equipped to face. In one of the classic passages from *War and Peace,* Tolstoy gives us an incomparable
image:

> Pierre did not in any way seek her approval, he merely
> studied her with interest. Formerly she had felt that he re-
> garded her with indifference and irony, and so had shrunk
> into herself as she did with others and had shown him only
> the combative side of her nature; but now he seemed to be
> trying to understand the most intimate places of her heart,
> and mistrustfully at first but afterwards gratefully, she let
> him see the hidden, kindly sides of her character.
>
> The most cunning man could not have crept into her
> confidence more successfully, evoking memories of the best
> times of her youth and showing sympathy with them. Yet
> Pierre's cunning consisted simply in finding pleasure in

drawing out the human qualities of the embittered, hard, and in her own way, proud princess.[107]

Eventually, she had found her time — and her deliverer.

The Communal Problems

My workplace ought to be and it's not.... It shouldn't be and it is.... My home would be okay except for....

What I want fixed or want to fix may be the answer to my deepest need. Or someone else's. I'll fight it to the last ditch, but it won't yield, this thing I have to eliminate in order to be happy. It will bully me around, if I'm lucky, to the point of ceasing my demands on it. Its wrongness will give me what its rightness never could. This does not mean that I am placidly accepting evil, even minor evil, or that I let myself be ground into the unhealthy soil of codependence.

But it does mean that the place in my heart from which I set out to heal and change is first given over to its own change. I recognize the self-interest which drives my zeal. I learn experientially the difference between good and evil zeal. What is being done in the community, the family, the job situation, and in me can be achieved only by the insoluble, by that with which we would interfere if we could master it.

Letting Go

We try to fit the problem into our demands, blinded by our own ideas of how it has to be fixed. People know when they have become a target, when they are the object of our emotional demands to change so that we can feel better, or in order to prove us right and them wrong. The quality of our demand sets up a reaction which makes change very difficult. It stiffens the resistance by aggravating the cause of the objectionable behavior in the first place.

But in prayer, in the desire to surrender to the impossible, we find solutions. What we had decided had to be there is slowly let go of and ceases to block the sight of a real solution — which may be less satisfactory and more effective.

What do I want more than the good of my brother or my sister?

What am I but the road on which they walk to God? What are they but my road into his heart?

Part VII

The Marble

Chapter 20

The Streak in the Marble

She had molded, carved, painted, and drawn his likeness. And in 1981, a few months before his death, Yrsa von Leistner, the eminent sculptress, completed a marble in which, with stunning skill, she portrayed the essence of this lonely man. Her stone has given us his features — sorrowful, meditative, and immensely dignified — but the rest of the head has not emerged from the marble. It is as if he has accepted his identity as prisoner, accepted what can never be changed, because, unknown to him, it has been transformed.

The marble disclosed an unexpected flaw — a red streak across the head and down its left side — harbinger of his imminent death. Both he and his wife traced its course with inquiring fingers. "Don't worry about him," a friend had told the sculptress. "If you told him he would die tomorrow, he'd be perfectly at peace. Not because he wants to escape this world, but because he is so eager to be with God."

Spandau was not the harshest part of Albert Speer's life: its sequel was. In the confused and difficult years which followed his release, he was to develop the lessons of Spandau.

Often, in the course of this book, I have had to say, "This happened. This is the way the redemptive process worked, even though he probably did not know it at the time." It's easy to reply, "Well, if he didn't know this, it didn't happen." But strangely enough, much of our salvation runs underground. It keeps its course in quietness, a steady current beneath the psychological landscape of human life.

So little does God ask. So eager is that river to catch up and carry the first subtle motions of our willingness to change. How familiar could we possibly be with its currents and its shoals? It runs in the dark, carrying our blunted desires, our defeats, our marred and inadequate victories. But the mighty fact of its embrace is sure, there beneath the suns and shadows on the surface of consciousness.

We live a mystery: how could we name each motion of its intent? Yet there is something that can be known, and I have said that in the spiritual academy of Spandau, I wished for Speer a good dose of St. Bernard. Perhaps he could not have made his way through the cultural and rhetorical thickets of twelfth-century theological discourse, but Cistercian optimism would have balanced the sterner theology from which he was drawing nourishment. Texts like these have much to reveal about what was going on beneath the surface of a life without event, and about that life later, when it began to acquire more event than perhaps it wanted.

> We have seen how every soul — even if burdened with sin, enmeshed in vice...a captive in exile...wandering and straying, filled with anxious forebodings and uneasy suspicions, a stranger in a hostile land...and counted with those who go down into hell — every soul, I say, standing thus under condemnation and without hope, has the power to turn and find it can not only breathe the fresh air of the hope of pardon and mercy, but also dare to aspire to the nuptials of the Word, not fearing to enter into alliance with God or to bear the sweet yoke of love with the King of angels.
>
> Why should it not venture with confidence into the presence of him by whose image it sees itself honored, and in whose likeness it knows itself made glorious? Why should it fear a majesty when its very origin gives it ground for confidence? All it has to do is to take care to preserve its natural purity by innocence of life, or rather to study to beautify and adorn with the brightness of its actions and dispositions the glorious beauty which is its birthright.[108]

There is nothing here about a point beyond which one has to be counted unforgivable, but instead a tranquil confidence in the redeeming process. "Innocence of life," of course, does not mean instant perfection. St. Bernard was a monk, and he knew monks spend their lives living out the practicalities of conversion.

Spandau made the man who was to face a world to which he seemed, at least to himself, stranger and outcast, pilgrim and exile. He told friends that he wished he could return to his monastery.

What happened after the last entry in the Spandau diaries? He went home, and it was not a home. It was awful. That was something to accept. He wrote books, and the fallout from that was something else to accept. We can earn a certain kind of redemption in our own eyes by taking public responsibility for the evil we have done. This can be an attempt to reenter the society we have violated, or to regain or reconstruct an image for ourselves. No one should be condemned for wanting this, for instinctively slipping this thread into the skein of motivation. If there was an amount of theatricality to Speer's presentation, I really don't know or care. Sooner or later, that kind of thing gets purified, to use the language of the old books.

For society does not always leap to accept one's invitation to forgive, and if the pose is all there is, the actor goes down to damaging reviews. Sometimes he goes down anyway. There has to be more. And there was. One of the stories from these years can serve to illustrate their character.

A Jewish woman, survivor of the death camps, who had married a German government official, found herself at a reception with Albert Speer. She said to him with remarkable courtesy, "Herr Speer, please forgive me. I hope you will understand that I cannot remain here." He replied quietly, "It is I who need your forgiveness, and I understand more than you think I do."

The world that met him personally, on TV or in his books, accepted or vilified his motives, rejected him as hypocritical or respected him as honest. But in all his encounters, he anticipated judgment.

"He had to have known...he must have known...."

What did these years feel like? What does acclamation feel like to someone who knows the tainted soil from which it grows? What was it like to reach out for a social rehabilitation he could not help wanting yet could never really believe in? Isolation, weariness, rebuff were as much a part of it as the unexpected interest in his books. He was damned by those who condemned as disloyalty his last minute repudiation of Hitler and damned by those who could never accept him onto the "other side."

"He had to have known...."

The sculptress who so accurately discerned the pathos and mystery of his life shared with him a profound spiritual friendship. He touched her trials with gentle wisdom, and in his need she was there to temper the force of his self-recrimination with acceptance and admiration. It is she who speaks of his "titanic personality," his sensibility and faithfulness. She calls him child-like, open, almost naive. Naive? You think of a few mistakes, beginning with Hitler. There was his enchantment with the British after the war when he innocently delivered over to them the documents which would provide evidence for his trial, and his misplaced trust in people who would turn against him. Perhaps yes, this worldly man was streaked with the unexpected naivete of a child.

What was it like to know that his friends had to take care to whom they spoke of him? A young Belgian couple who shared and understood his love for God must have solaced the emptiness left by his alienated children. But they could not speak much of him to others. This Nazi, this Speer...

"He had to have known...."

We know of a late love affair, discovered of course and sensationalized by the press. Was it something of a full circle? I cannot help but think again of the child. From a wrecked marriage, from the torments of isolation and self-rejection, did he look out on the mother figure, coming at last to an abandoned child, a concrete experience of the forgiveness long given but emotionally unknown? I know what can be said, and I would have preferred another way. But though I don't defend, neither am I disposed to judge.

We have the marble. It is something to contemplate, for it gives to the world he so badly damaged a sublime meditation on the mystery of the redemption.

"My merit is the mercy of the Lord."[109]

Notes

1. Albert Speer, *Inside the Third Reich* (New York: Macmillan Co., 1970), 375–76. Hereafter, referred to as *Memoirs*.

2. Albert Speer, *Spandau, The Secret Diaries* (New York: Macmillan Co., 1976), 3. Hereafter referred to as *Diaries*.

3. Leo Tolstoy, *War and Peace* (Chicago: Encyclopaedia Britannica, Great Books ed., 1952), 639.

4. *Diaries*, xi–xii.

5. *Memoirs*, 488–89.

6. *Diaries*, 11.

7. *Memoirs*, 219.

8. Walter Abbott, ed., *Documents of Vatican II* (New York: America Press, 1966), "The Church in the Modern World," no. 22, pp. 220–21. Hereafter referred to as "Modern World."

9. John Paul II, *The Mercy of God* (Boston: St. Paul Editions, 1981), no. 13, p. 40. Hereafter referred to as *Mercy*.

10. "Modern World," no. 41, p. 240.

11. *Mercy*, no. 6, p. 23.

12. *Memoirs*, 114.

13. *Diaries*, 38.

14. Ibid., 211.

15. Ibid., 5.

16. *Memoirs*, 31.

17. Ibid., 32.

18. *Diaries*, 154.

19. *Memoirs*, 195.

20. Ibid., 197.

21. Ibid., 32.

22. Ibid., 64.

23. Ibid., 375.

24. Ibid., 136.

25. Ibid., 111–13.

26. Ibid., 112–13.

27. Ibid., 112.

28. Ibid., 291.

29. Ibid., 334.

30. Ibid., 339.
31. Ibid., 403.
32. Ibid., 442.
33. Ibid., 513.
34. *Modern World,* no. 22, pp. 221–22.
35. *Memoirs,* 485.
36. Ibid., 116.
37. *Diaries,* 121.
38. *Mercy,* no. 7, p. 26.
39. *Diaries,* 179.
40. Ibid., 340.
41. Ibid., 341.
42. Ibid., 335.
43. *Memoirs,* 523–24.
44. *Diaries,* 375.
45. Ibid., 142.
46. Ibid., 419–20.
47. Tolstoy, *War and Peace,* 340.
48. *Diaries,* 154.
49. Ibid., 348.
50. *Mercy,* no. 6, pp. 22–23.
51. *Diaries,* 317.
52. Ibid., 26.
53. Ibid., 71.
54. Ibid., 26.
55. Ibid., 12.
56. Ibid., 113–114.
57. *Memoirs,* Foreword.
58. Antiphon at the Song of Zachary on Easter morning.
59. *Diaries,* 68–69.
60. Ibid., 27.
61. Ibid., 50.
62. Ibid., 45.
63. Ibid., 185.
64. Ibid., 349.
65. Ibid., 109.
66. Ibid., 378–79.
67. Ibid., 10.
68. Ibid., 150.
69. Ibid., 178.
70. Ibid., 354.
71. *Memoirs,* 484.

72. See Eric Sevareid, *Not So Wild a Dream* (New York: Atheneum, 1976), xiii.

73. *Memoirs,* 512.

74. *Diaries,* 74.

75. Ibid., 34.

76. Ibid., 264.

77. Ibid., 333.

78. Ibid., 337.

79. Ibid.

80. Ibid., 74.

81. Ibid., 76.

82. Ibid., 121.

83. Ibid., 254–55.

84. Ibid., 259.

85. Ibid., 268.

86. Ibid., 276.

87. Ibid., 259.

88. Ibid., 286.

89. Ibid., 268–69.

90. Ibid., 371.

91. Ibid., 204.

92. Ibid., 240.

93. Ibid., 204–5.

94. Ibid., 250.

95. Ibid., 227.

96. Ibid.

97. Ibid., 226.

98. Ibid., 277.

99. Ibid., 275.

100. Ibid., 220.

101. Ibid., 305.

102. Ibid., 24–25.

103. Ibid., 440.

104. Ibid., 396.

105. Ibid., 397.

106. Ibid., 420.

107. Tolstoy, *War and Peace,* 631–32.

108. Bernard of Clairvaux, *Sermons on the Song of Songs,* vol. 4 (Kalamazoo, Mich.: Cistercian Publications, 1980), Sermon 83, 1.

109. Bernard of Clairvaux, *Sermons on the Song of Songs,* vol. 3 (Kalamazoo, Mich.: Cistercian Publications, 1979), Sermon 61, 5.